MW01706092

Que® Quick Reference Series

1-2-3® for Windows™ Quick Reference

Rosemary Colonna

Que®

1-2-3 for Windows Quick Reference.

Copyright ©1992 by Que Corporation.

All rights reserved. Printed in the United States of America. No part of this book may be used or reproduced in any form or by any means, or stored in a database or retrieval system, without prior written permission of the publisher except in the case of brief quotations embodied in critical articles and reviews. Making copies of any part of this book for any purpose other than your own personal use is a violation of United States copyright laws. For information, address Que Corporation, 11711 North College Avenue, Suite 140, Carmel, IN 46032.

Library of Congress Catalog Number: 91-62304

ISBN: 0-88022-783-4

This book is sold *as is*, without warranty of any kind, either express or implied, respecting the contents of this book, including but not limited to implied warranties for the book's quality, performance, merchantability, or fitness for any particular purpose. Neither Que Corporation nor its dealers or distributors shall be liable to the purchaser or any other person or entity with respect to any liability, loss, or damage caused or alleged to be caused directly or indirectly by this book.

94 93 92 91 4 3 2 1

Interpretation of the printing code: the rightmost double-digit number is the year of the book's printing; the rightmost single-digit number is the number of the book's printing. For example, a printing code of 92-4 shows that the fourth printing of the book occurred in 1992.

This book is based on Lotus 1-2-3 for Windows Version 1.0.

Que Quick Reference Series

The *Que Quick Reference Series* is a portable resource of essential microcomputer knowledge. Drawing on the experience of many of Que's best-selling authors, this series helps you easily access important program information. The *Que Quick Reference Series* includes these titles:

1-2-3 for DOS Release 2.3 Quick Reference
1-2-3 for DOS Release 3.1+ Quick Reference
1-2-3 for Windows Quick Reference
1-2-3 Release 2.2 Quick Reference
Allways Quick Reference
AutoCAD Quick Reference, 2nd Edition
Batch Files and Macros Quick Reference
CheckFree Quick Reference
CorelDRAW! Quick Reference
dBASE IV Quick Reference
Excel for Windows Quick Reference
Fastback Quick Reference
Hard Disk Quick Reference
Harvard Graphics Quick Reference
LapLink Quick Reference
Microsoft Word 5 Quick Reference
Microsoft Word Quick Reference
Microsoft Works Quick Reference
MS-DOS 5 Quick Reference
MS-DOS Quick Reference
Norton Utilities Quick Reference
Paradox Quick Reference
PC Tools 7 Quick Reference
Q&A 4 Quick Reference
Quark XPress Quick Reference
Quattro Pro Quick Reference
Quicken Quick Reference
System 7 Quick Reference
UNIX Programmer's Quick Reference
UNIX Shell Commands Quick Reference
Windows 3 Quick Reference
WordPerfect 5.1 Quick Reference
WordPerfect for Windows Quick Reference
WordPerfect Quick Reference

Publisher

Lloyd J. Short

Series Director

Karen A. Bluestein

Production Editor

Cindy Morrow

Editor

Jill D. Bond

Technical Editor

Joyce Nielsen

Production Team

Claudia Bell
Brad Chinn
Brook Farling
Dennis Clay Hager
Betty Kish
Bob LaRoche
Juli Pavey
Joe Ramon
Susan VandeWalle
Johnna VanHoose

Trademark Acknowledgments

1-2-3 and Lotus are registered trademarks and Allways is a trademark of Lotus Development Corporation.

Microsoft is a registered trademark and Windows is a trademark of Microsoft Corporation.

Table of Contents

Introduction

1-2-3 for Windows Quick Reference is not a rehash of traditional documentation and is not intended to replace the 1-2-3 user documentation. Instead, this quick reference is a compilation of the most frequently used functions and commands from 1-2-3 for Windows. If you are new to 1-2-3 for Windows, you can complement this quick reference with Que's *Using 1-2-3 for Windows,* Special Edition.

1-2-3 for Windows Quick Reference includes the quick reference information that you need as you create, edit, display, and print 1-2-3 for Windows spreadsheets that range from simple to complex. Organized alphabetically by task, this book places essential 1-2-3 for Windows information at your fingertips.

1-2-3 for Windows Quick Reference is divided into alphabetized sections by command. Three separate command references—one each for the Main Menu, Graph Window, and Transcript Window—lead you step-by-step through the commands and procedures for using 1-2-3 for Windows like a pro!

Now you can put essential information at your fingertips with *1-2-3 for Windows Quick Reference*—and the entire Que Quick Reference Series!

HINTS FOR USING THIS BOOK

As you read this book, keep the following conventions in mind:

A **+** between keys in a key combination indicates that you press and hold the first key and press the next key. A **–** between keys in a key combination indicates that you press and release the first key, and then press the next key. Words that you type and keys you press appear in **boldface blue** type.

To select menu options and commands with the mouse, move the pointer to the option or command and click. To select options and commands with the keyboard, press the keys that are **boldfaced** and **blue**.

Information that you see on-screen appears in a `special` typeface.

1-2-3 FOR WINDOWS BASICS

1-2-3 for Windows is an advanced spreadsheet that contains complete spreadsheet publishing and presentation features. 1-2-3 for Windows uses the Microsoft Windows Graphical User Interface (GUI) and maintains compatibility with other releases of 1-2-3.

You can use 1-2-3 for Windows commands to enhance the appearance of data, perform calculations with formulas and @functions, chart data and create graphics, add text to a worksheet, use data in multiple worksheet files, perform calculations, analyze data, perform "what if" analysis, and use macros to automate routine tasks.

The 1-2-3 for Windows Screen

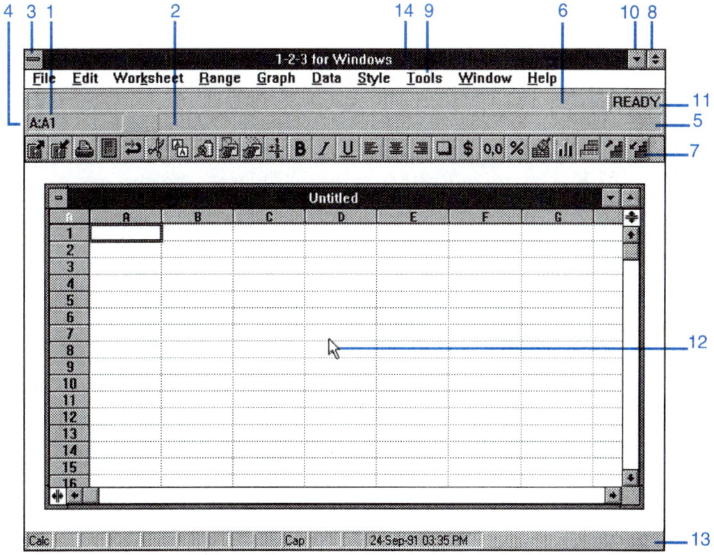

The 1-2-3 for Windows screen is comprised of the following elements:

1. Address box—Area of the edit line that displays the location of the current cell.
2. Contents box—Section of the edit line that displays the contents of the current cell.
3. Control menu box—Contains commands that enable you to restore, move, minimize, and maximize the window. This box is located in the upper left corner of the screen. Click with the mouse to display the Control menu. The commands appear dimmed when they are not available. Every window contains a separate Control menu.
4. Control panel—Area at the top of the screen that contains the title bar, menu bar, format line, and edit line.
5. Edit line—Section of the screen where data is entered or edited. The edit line contains the address box and the contents box.
6. Format line—Contains the mode indicator and displays the format description of the current cell.
7. Icon palette—SmartIcons (icon buttons) that enable you to access commonly used commands and macros.
8. Maximize/Restore button—Enlarges the current window to the size of the full screen or restores a maximized window to its previous size.
9. Menu bar—Horizontal bar containing the 1-2-3 for Windows commands. These commands always appear on-screen.
10. Minimize button—Reduces the current window to the size of an icon.
11. Mode indicator—Appears in the format line and indicates the current state of 1-2-3 for Windows.
12. Mouse pointer—Indicates screen location of next mouse action. The shape of the mouse pointer varies depending on the task being performed.

13. Status indicators—Appear in the status line when you press specific keys or when 1-2-3 performs specific tasks.

14. Status line—Area at the bottom of the screen where the status indicators and current date and time appear.

Types of 1-2-3 Windows

The screen appearance has changed in 1-2-3 for Windows. The following list describes the new windows found in 1-2-3 for Windows.

Window	*Function*
1-2-3	Contains the entire 1-2-3 for Windows application. With the exception of the Help window, all other windows open within this window.
Worksheet	Automatically opens when 1-2-3 for Windows is started. Contains the worksheet file.
Graph	Enables you to view and enhance graphs.
Help	Displays context-sensitive on-line help.
1-2-3 Classic	Displays 1-2-3 Release 3.1 menus as an alternative to the 1-2-3 for Windows menus.
Macro Trace	Enables you to debug 1-2-3 macros. Displays current location and instructions of a macro while it runs.
Print Preview	Shows how the worksheet will appear when printed.

Window	*Function*
Transcript	Enables you to copy or cut and paste the recorded keystrokes when creating a macro. Enables you to run a macro directly.

1-2-3 KEYS

You can use specific keys on the keyboard to perform special 1-2-3 operations. You use the accelerator keys, for example, to perform tasks that you also can complete using a menu command. The following section defines the various keys and describes the operations for which they are used.

Pointer Keys

Pointer keys move the cell pointer within worksheets, across worksheets in a file, and across active files. Many pointer keys also move the cursor while in EDIT mode. Press the **Num Lock** key to toggle between pointer-movement mode and 10-key entry mode.

For key combinations, such as **Shift**+**Tab**, press and hold the first key; then press the second key. A plus sign between key names means you must hold the first key while pressing the second key.

Pointer keys used with one worksheet

Key	*Function*
←	Moves the cell pointer left one cell.
→	Moves the cell pointer right one cell.
↑	Moves the cell pointer up one row.
↓	Moves the cell pointer down one row.

Key	*Function*
Ctrl+← or **Shift+Tab**	Moves the cell pointer one screen to the left.
Ctrl+→ or **Tab**	Moves the cell pointer one screen to the right.
End+←	Moves the cell pointer to the left.*
End+→	Moves the cell pointer to the right.*
End+↑	Moves the cell pointer up.*
End+↓	Moves the cell pointer down.*
End+Home	Moves the cell pointer to the lowest right corner of the active area.
Home	Moves the cell pointer to the upper left corner of the worksheet. If worksheet titles are fixed, moves the cell pointer to the upper left unfixed cell.
Num Lock	Toggles the numeric keypad between pointer movement and numeric entry.
PgUp	Moves the cell pointer up one worksheet screen.
PgDn	Moves the cell pointer down one worksheet screen.
F5(GoTo)	Prompts you for a cell address or range name; then moves the cell pointer directly to that cell, which can be in another worksheet or file.
F6(Window)	If the window is split, moves the cell pointer to the next window, which can be in another worksheet or file.

Key	*Function*
Scroll Lock	Toggles the scroll function on and off; when on, the entire window moves when you press one of the arrow keys.

*Moves the cell pointer in the direction of the arrow to the next intersection of a blank cell and a cell that contains data.

Pointer keys used with multiple worksheets

Key	*Function*
Ctrl-PgUp	Moves the cell pointer to the next worksheet.
Ctrl-PgDn	Moves the cell pointer to the preceding worksheet.
Ctrl-Home	Moves the cell pointer to the home position in the first worksheet in the file (usually cell A:A1).
End+Ctrl-Home	Moves the cell pointer to the end of the active area for the file in the last worksheet.
End+Ctrl-PgUp or **End+Ctrl-PgDn**	Moves the cell pointer through the worksheets to the next intersection of a blank cell and a cell that contains data.
Ctrl-End+ Ctrl-PgUp	Moves the cell pointer to the next file.
Ctrl-End+ Ctrl-PgDn	Moves the cell pointer to the preceding file.
Ctrl-End+Home	Moves the cell pointer to the first file in memory.
Ctrl-End+End	Moves the cell pointer to the last file in memory.

Function Keys

Function keys save you time as you perform special tasks. Some keyboards have 12 (or more) function keys. 1-2-3 uses only the first 10, which are labeled F1 through F10.

To expand the available function keys, 1-2-3 combines **Alt** or **Ctrl** with some function keys. Following is a list of function keys and function key combinations:

Keys	*Name*	*Function*
F1	Help	Opens the Help window and accesses the on-line help facility.
F2	Edit	Places 1-2-3 in EDIT mode so that you can change the current cell.
F3	Name	Causes a list of names to appear when a command or formula accepts a range name or file name. A list of functions appears when you type @ into a formula. A list of macro key names and advanced macro commands appears when you type a left brace ({) in a label.
F4	Abs	In READY mode, anchors the cell pointer and enables you to specify a range. In EDIT, POINT, and VALUE modes, changes a cell or range reference in a formula from relative to absolute to mixed.

Keys	*Name*	*Function*
F5	GoTo	Moves the cell pointer to a specific cell or a named range, another worksheet in the same file, or another active file.
F6	Pane	Controls movement of the cell pointer between worksheet panes created with the **W**indow **S**plit **H**orizontal and **W**indow **S**plit **V**ertical command options.
F7	Query	In READY mode, repeats the last **D**ata **Q**uery command. Switches between FIND and READY modes during a **D**ata **Q**uery **F**ind operation.
F8	Table	Repeats the last Data What-if Table command.
F9	Calc	Recalculates all formulas, including those that refer to worksheet files on disk.
F10	Menu	Activates the menu bar (equivalent to **Alt**).
Alt-F1	Compose	Creates characters that cannot be typed directly from the keyboard.
Alt-F2	Step	Toggles macro STEP mode on and off in the Macro Trace window.
Alt-F3	Run	Lists macros that are available to run.

Keys	*Name*	*Function*
Alt-F6	Zoom	Enlarges the current pane to the full size of the window or returns the pane to its original size.
Alt-F7 **Alt-F8** **Alt-F9**	Add-in 1 Add-in 2 Add-in 3	Starts 1-2-3 add-ins that are assigned to respective keys.

Accelerator Keys

You can use the combination of certain keys to perform tasks that you also can complete using menu commands. This section defines the accelerator keys and specifies equivalent commands.

Key	*Function*
Alt-Backspace	Reverses the most recently executed command or action. Equivalent to **E**dit **U**ndo.
Alt-F4	Terminates a 1-2-3 session and returns you to the Windows Program Manager after saving any unsaved files. Equivalent to the **F**ile **E**xit command.
Ctrl-F4	When used to close an active window, enables you to save the file when it contains unsaved changes. Equivalent to selecting **F**ile **C**lose when the active window is a Worksheet window. Equivalent to selecting **C**lose from the Control menu of a Worksheet window.

Key	*Function*
Ctrl-F6	Cycles through open Worksheet, Graph, or Transcript windows. Equivalent to selecting Next from the Control menu of a Worksheet, Graph, or Transcript window.
Ctrl-Ins	Copies selected data and formatting from the worksheet to the Clipboard. Equivalent to the Edit Copy command.
Ctrl-letter	Runs the macro associated with the letter name. Equivalent to Tools Macro Run.
Del	Deletes selected data and related formatting. Does not move deleted material to the Clipboard. Equivalent to Edit Clear.
Shift-Ins	Copies data and formatting from the Clipboard to specified locations in the worksheet. Equivalent to Edit Paste.
Shift-Del	Moves selected data and related formatting from the worksheet to the Clipboard. Equivalent to Edit Cut.

USING A MOUSE

You can use a mouse to highlight ranges, select commands, maneuver objects on-screen, and select SmartIcons from the icon palette.

Terminology

You need to understand the following terms when using a mouse.

Term	*Action*
Click	Press and release the mouse button quickly.
Double-click	Press and release the mouse button twice in rapid succession.
Drag	Press and hold the mouse button while moving the mouse.
Point	Position the mouse pointer on an object or item on-screen.

Mouse Pointers

When you use the mouse, symbols appear on-screen to indicate the section of the screen that the next action of the mouse will affect. The mouse pointer changes shape depending on the task performed at a specified location. The following list describes the tasks and the respective mouse pointer shapes:

Pointer Shape	*Tasks*
White arrow	Selects cells and ranges.
White two-headed arrow	Resizes windows.
I-beam	Enters and edits data.
Black two-headed vertical arrow	Resizes rows, creates or resizes a horizontal pane.
Black two-headed horizontal arrow	Resizes columns, creates or resizes a vertical pane.

Pointer Shape	*Tasks*
Thin black cross	Positions objects in graphs.
Hourglass	Indicates a wait period, which enables 1-2-3 to finish performing a task.
Pencil	Creates freehand drawings in graphs.
Hand	Moves objects in graphs.
Pointing hand	In Help, displays a definition or goes to a cross-reference.
Pointed finger	Selects objects in graphs.

SELECTING MENU ITEMS

You can select a menu item using the keyboard or the mouse. The second line in the Worksheet window is the *menu bar*, which is where available menu selections appear.

To select a command using the keyboard

1. Press **Alt** or **F10** (Menu) to activate the menu bar.
2. Press the underlined letter in the menu to highlight the command that you want to select.

   You also can press → and ← to highlight the underlined letter.
3. Press **Enter** when the command is highlighted.
4. Repeat steps 2 and 3 to select the next section of the command from the pull-down menu.

   You also can use the ↑ and ↓ keys to move within the pull-down and cascade menus.

To select a command using the mouse

1. Press **Alt** or **F10** (Menu) to activate the menu bar.

2. Move the mouse pointer to the command that you want to select.
3. Click on the command.

Notes

When you select a command that contains an ellipsis (...), a dialog box appears with more choices that pertain to the menu command. A solid triangle indicates that an additional (cascade) menu will appear.

Dimmed commands on the menus are not available for selection. Commands are dimmed when they are not applicable for the specific task that you are performing.

USING DIALOG BOXES

The following elements appear in the 1-2-3 for Windows dialog boxes:

Box	*Function*
Text box	Enables you to enter and edit data.
List box	Displays available choices.
Information box	Contains information about the selected file.
Drop-down box	Enables you to scroll forward or backward and select one of several dialog box options.
Option button	Enables you to select a specific dialog box option.
Command button	Enables you to perform an action.

To select an option or command with the keyboard, press **Alt** and the underlined letter of the command you want. To move to the option you want, press **Tab** or **Shift-Tab**, then press **Enter**.

To select an option or command with the mouse, click the desired option or command.

Pressing **Enter** is usually the fastest way to accept dialog settings, close the dialog box, and execute a menu command. Pressing **Esc** always selects the **C**ancel command button, which cancels your dialog settings and closes the dialog box.

STARTING 1-2-3 FOR WINDOWS

To start 1-2-3 for Windows, you must be in the Microsoft Windows 3.0 environment. Follow these steps:

1. Start Windows.
2. Open the Windows Program Manager.
3. Select and open the group window that contains 1-2-3 for Windows.
4. To select 1-2-3 for Windows, double-click on the application icon for 1-2-3 for Windows or press the arrow keys to highlight the 1-2-3 for Windows icon. Then press **Enter**.

USING THE ICON PALETTE

The icon palette consists of a set of SmartIcons that enables you to access commonly used commands and macros. You cannot access SmartIcons from the keyboard. You must click the specified icon with the mouse.

The **T**ools **I**con **P**alette command enables you to change the position of the icon palette in the 1-2-3 window, change available icons, hide (remove from the screen) the icon palette, and assign macros to custom icons. A description of the selected SmartIcon appears on-screen when you click on the icon with the right mouse button.

ENTERING AND EDITING DATA

A spreadsheet cell can hold up to 512 characters. When typing characters that are to be entered into a cell, the characters appear in a Contents box. The I-beam pointer indicates where the next character will appear. After you make certain that the entry is correct, confirm the entry by pressing **Enter** or by clicking the Confirm button. The entry appears in the cell.

1-2-3 determines the type of entry you are typing and either LABEL or VALUE appears as the mode indicator. If the cell entry is a number or formula, 1-2-3 displays VALUE. If the cell entry is text, 1-2-3 displays LABEL.

Entering Labels

If the label starts with one of the following numeric characters

0 1 2 3 4 5 6 7 8 9 . + - $ (@ #

you first must type a label prefix. The label prefix tells 1-2-3 that the entry you are typing is a label and indicates how the text should be aligned in the cell. 1-2-3 considers the entry a value if you type a label that begins with one of these numeric characters without using a label prefix.

Following are the label prefixes that you can use to control alignment:

Label Prefix	*Function*
' (apostrophe)	Aligns label to the left (default setting).
" (quotation mark)	Aligns label to the right.
^ (caret)	Centers label in the cell.

Label Prefix	*Function*
\ (backslash)	Repeats a character to fill a cell.
| (vertical bar)	Aligns label to the left and does not print it.

Entering Numbers

To enter a number, type one of the following characters:

0 1 2 3 4 5 6 7 8 9 . + – $

To attach a note to a number, type

; (semicolon)

after the number; then type the note.

Entering Formulas

To enter a formula, you must start the entry with one of the following numbers or symbols:

0 1 2 3 4 5 6 7 8 9 . + – $ (@ #

If you start the entry with any other character, 1-2-3 assumes that the entry is a label.

Use operators to specify the calculations that 1-2-3 is to perform. To change the order of precedence (the order in which operators are evaluated), use parentheses.

To attach a note to a number, type

; (semicolon)

after the number; then type the note.

Numeric formulas operate on numbers, string formulas operate on text, and logical formulas compare two entries. The result of a logical test is TRUE or FALSE. TRUE has a value of 1 and FALSE has a value of 0.

Following is a list of items included in formulas:

Item	*Description*
@functions	Predefined formulas
Addresses	Cell addresses or range names
Operators	Symbols, such as + and –, for numeric, string, or logical operations
Numbers	Used for math calculations
Strings	Text used in string formulas

Following is a list of numeric operators listed in order of precedence:

Operator	*Meaning*
^	Exponentiation
+, –	Positive, Negative
*, /	Multiplication, Division
+, –	Addition, Subtraction
=, <>	Equal, Not equal
<, >	Less than, Greater than
<=	Less than or equal to
>=	Greater than or equal to
#NOT#	Reverses a true/false result
#AND#	Logical AND
#OR#	Logical OR
&	Concatenates a string to the preceding string

Enclose the operation in parentheses to override the order of precedence. Operations inside the parentheses are performed first.

Editing Cell Contents

Use the following procedures to edit the contents of cells.

To make corrections as you type an entry

Press **F2** (Edit) or **Backspace** as you are typing to correct an error. To correct an existing cell entry, press **F2** (Edit).

Replacing a short entry

Ignore the contents of the cell you are editing and type a new entry. Press **Enter**, click the Confirm button, or click another cell to replace the old entry with the new entry. Press **Esc** before pressing **Enter** to keep the original entry and cancel the new entry.

To edit contents of a cell or text box

1. Select the cell or text box you want to edit.
2. Switch to EDIT mode by pressing **F2** (Edit), double-clicking the cell, or clicking anywhere in the Contents box.
3. Type the | (vertical bar) or insert the cell pointer (I-beam) where you want to begin editing.
4. Press **Del** or **Backspace** to erase the selected characters. Press and hold the mouse button and drag to select characters to be erased.
5. Type the new characters.
6. Press **Enter**, click the Confirm button, or click another cell to confirm the entry.

CONTROL MENU COMMANDS

The Control commands manipulate the size and placement of all windows and dialog boxes within 1-2-3 for Windows.

To access the Control menu, click the box that is in the top left corner of the 1-2-3 window, click the dialog box, or press **Alt-space bar**.

To access the Control menu of a window that is currently open, click the box in the top left corner of the 1-2-3 window or press **Alt--**(hyphen).

To access the Control menu of a window that is displayed as an icon, click the icon or press **Alt--** (hyphen).

ACCESSING HELP

1-2-3 for Windows provides an on-line Help function that appears in its own window. You can open, close, resize, or move the Help window.

To access Help, press **F1**. You can access Help from anywhere within the program. The Help function contains information that is not available in the printed documentation.

The Help icon bar appears at the top of the window and contains five Help buttons. To access a button, click with the mouse or press the underlined letter.

The Help Window can remain open only while you are working in a Worksheet, Graph, or Transcript window.

MAIN MENU COMMAND REFERENCE

This Command Reference includes the 1-2-3 for Windows commands that you can access from the Main menu. This section is organized the same way for each command. First, the Purpose of the command is listed. The Purpose is followed by specific procedures for using the command. Finally, a Notes section contains additional comments, information, hints, and suggestions for using the command.

Data Connect to External

Purpose

Connects 1-2-3 with an external database table and assigns a range name to the table.

To connect 1-2-3 to an external database

1. Select Data Connect to External by clicking the mouse or pressing **Alt+D+C** from the keyboard.
2. Connect to the driver by double-clicking a driver name from the list box or entering a driver name in the text box from the keyboard.
3. Connect to the database by double-clicking a database name from the list box or entering a database name in the text box from the keyboard.
4. Connect to the table by double-clicking a table name from the list box or entering a table name in the text box from the keyboard.
5. Create a range name for the table.
6. Select the **C**onnect button.
7. Select **OK**.

Note

The table name appears as the default range name. If this range name was already used in the current worksheet, 1-2-3 for Windows displays ???? (question marks) instead of a default name.

Data Distribution

Purpose

Creates a frequency distribution table showing how often specific data appears in a database.

Reminders

Data must be numeric and arranged in a column, row, or rectangular range located in one or more worksheet files, either open or on disk. This is called the *value range*.

Labels or blanks cells cannot be included in the bin range.

To create a frequency distribution table

1. Move the cell pointer to a worksheet portion that has two adjacent blank columns. In the left column, enter the highest value for each entry in the bin range. Enter these bin values in ascending order.

2. Select the **V**alues range, which contains the data being analyzed.

3. Select Data Distribution by clicking the mouse or pressing **Alt**+**D**+**D** from the keyboard.

4. Enter the **B**in range by either selecting the range or entering the range address or name.

Note

The frequency column extends one row beyond the bin range to represent the number of values that exceeds the largest value in the bin range.

Data External Options Create Table

Purpose

Creates the structure for a new external database based on the structure of a 1-2-3 database or another external database.

To create a structure for an external database

1. Select Data External Options Create Table by clicking with the mouse or pressing **Alt**+**D**+**E**+**C** from the keyboard.

2. Select the driver name (such as dBASE_IV or Paradox) from the list; then select **C**onnect.

3. Specify the path where you want to store the new database file; then select **C**onnect.

4. Type the name for the new database; then select **C**onnect.

5. If the range name that 1-2-3 assigns to the database is acceptable, select **C**onnect; otherwise, enter a new name.

6. In the **M**odel range text box, specify the range of the 1-2-3 database or type the range name of the external database.

7. In the **O**utput range text box, specify the first cell in which the table definition is placed.

8. Select **OK**.

Data External Options Disconnect

Purpose

Breaks the connection to an external database. Use this command when you no longer need to access the database.

To break the connection to an external database

1. Select Data External Options Disconnect by clicking with the mouse or pressing **Alt+D+E+I** from the keyboard.

2. From the list of Co**n**nected Tables, select the name of the external database to disconnect.

3. Select **OK**.

Data External Options Paste Fields

Purpose

Inserts a table of information about the fields in an external database. You then can use this information to set up criteria and output ranges for data queries.

To insert a table of information

1. Position the cell pointer where you want the field information pasted.
2. Select Data External Options Paste Fields by clicking with the mouse or pressing **Alt+D+E+P** from the keyboard.
3. Select a name from the list of Connected Tables.
4. Select the Range text box and specify the range.
5. Select **OK**.

Data External Options Send Command

Purpose

Issues a driver-specific command to an external database that is connected to the current file. For example, you can send a command to dBASE that indicates which index file to use.

To use Data External Options Send Command

1. Select Data External Options Send Command by clicking with the mouse or pressing **Alt+D+E+S** from the keyboard.
2. From the Connect to driver list, select a driver; then select Connect.
3. Specify the database name in the Connect to database field.

Data Fill

Purpose

Fills a specified range with a series of equally incremented numbers, dates, times, or percentages.

To fill a specified range

1. Specify the range to be filled.
2. Select Data Fill by clicking the mouse or pressing **Alt+D+F** from the keyboard.
3. Use the Range text box to change the range or accept the existing range.
4. Enter the Start number, date, or time. You can reference a cell or range that results in a value. The default value is 0.
5. When a Step value is requested, type the positive or negative number by which you want the value to be incremented. Date or time Step values can use special units. The default value is 1.
6. Enter a Stop value. The default value is 8191.
7. Select **OK**.

Note

Numbers generated by Data Fill overwrite previous entries.

Data Matrix

Purpose

Inverts columns and rows in square matrices or multiplies column-and-row matrices of cells.

Reminder

The output range created is the same size as the matrix being inverted or multiplied and will write over existing data in that range. Make sure that the output range is blank or contains data that can be overwritten.

To invert a matrix

1. Select the matrix to invert.

   The matrix can contain up to 80 columns and 80 rows and must have the same number of columns and rows. The matrix range can exist in any file, whether it is active or on disk.

2. Select Data Matrix Invert by clicking the mouse or pressing Alt+D+M+I from the keyboard.

3. Use the From text box to change the matrix range or accept the existing range.

4. Use the To text box to designate the range that is going to contain the results.

   You can only specify either the first cell in the range or the entire range.

5. Select OK.

To multiply matrices

1. Select the range of the first matrix to be multiplied.

2. Select Data Matrix Multiply by clicking the mouse or pressing Alt+D+M+M from the keyboard.

3. Use the First matrix text box to change the matrix range or accept the existing range.

4. Select the range for the second matrix using the Second matrix text box by highlighting the matrix or entering the range address or name from the keyboard.

5. Designate the range for the output matrix using the Output matrix text box.

6. Select OK.

Notes

Any matrix of values up to a maximum of 80 rows and 80 columns can be multiplied by 1-2-3 for Windows. The range can be contained in any file whether it is active or on disk.

Only the first cell in the range needs to be specified.

Data Parse

Purpose

Separates a single column of long labels into distinct text and numeric cell entries arranged into multiple columns.

To separate a column of long labels into cell entries

1. Select the **I**nput column, which contains the range where you want to begin parsing data.
2. Select Data Parse by clicking the mouse or pressing **Alt+D+P** from the keyboard.
3. Select **C**reate to insert a new row into the worksheet at the location of the cell pointer. The format line is entered in the new row.
4. Select the **F**ormat line to scroll through the line and verify that it represents the data in the line below it.
5. Edit the format line if there are differences between the data and the format.
6. Use the **O**utput range text box to specify the range where 1-2-3 will place the parsed data.
7. Select **OK**.

Note

Use **R**eset to clear the **I**nput column and **O**utput range text boxes.

Data Query Criteria Range

Purpose

Uses specified criteria to locate and edit selected records in a 1-2-3 database or external table.

To locate and edit selected records

1. Specify or highlight the range that will contain field names and criteria. The range must contain at least two rows: the first row includes field names from the top row of the database that you want to search, and the subsequent row(s) includes the criteria you specify that defines which records 1-2-3 will select from the database.

2. Select Data Query Criteria by clicking the mouse or pressing Alt+D+Q+C from the keyboard.

Note

Values, labels, formulas, @functions, or logical or relational expressions are *criteria.*

Data Query Delete

Purpose

Removes from the input range any records that meet conditions in the criteria range.

"Cleans up" your database by removing records that are not current or that you extracted to another worksheet.

To use Data Query Delete

1. Select Data Query by clicking the mouse or pressing Alt+D+Q from the keyboard.

2. Use the Input range text box to specify the input range.

3. Use the Criteria range text box to specify the criteria range. 1-2-3 selects all records if no criteria is specified under the field names.

4. Select Delete.

5. Either select Delete to complete the Data Query Delete or select Cancel to cancel the command and return to the Data Query dialog box.

Notes

You must define a 1-2-3 database complete with input and criterion ranges.

Only one database can be specified as the input range.

Before any records are deleted, a warning message appears.

Data Query Extract/Extract Unique Only

Purpose

Data Query Extract copies to the output range of the worksheet records that meet conditions set in the criteria. Data Query Extract unique only copies only nonduplicate records and sorts them.

To use Data Query Extract

Select Data Query Extract by clicking the mouse or pressing Alt+D+Q+E from the keyboard to copy all records that meet the conditions set in the criteria to a defined Output range.

To use Data Query Extract unique only

Select Data Query Extract unique only by clicking the mouse or pressing Alt+D+Q+U from the keyboard to copy nonduplicate records that meet conditions set in the criteria and to sort the copied records. After you select the Extract unique only check box, select Extract to complete the command.

Note

You must define a 1-2-3 database complete with input, output, and criterion ranges.

Data Query Find

Purpose

Finds records in the database that meet conditions you set in the criterion range and highlights them.

To find specified records in a database

1. Designate the **I**nput range by entering the address or range name of the database or highlighting the range.
2. Select Data Query by clicking the mouse or pressing **Alt**+**D**+**Q** from the keyboard.
3. Designate a criteria range by highlighting it or entering the address or range name.
4. Select **F**ind.

   The cell pointer highlights the first record that meets the criteria. You hear a beep if no record in the input range meets the criteria.
5. Press ↑ or ↓ to move to the next record that meets the criteria. Press **Home** or **End** to find the first or last record in the database that meets the criteria.
6. You can edit contents within a record. When the cell pointer highlights the cell you want to edit, press **F2** and edit the cell contents. Press **Enter**.

   You can end **D**ata **Q**uery **F**ind, leaving the cell pointer in the current cell in the current record and return to READY mode by pressing **F7**.

Note

Data Query Find works only with a single input range. You cannot use external tables or multiple input ranges.

Data Query Input Range

Purpose

Specifies a range of data records to be searched.

To specify a range of data records to search

1. Select Data Query Input range by clicking the mouse or pressing **Alt+D+Q+I** from the keyboard.
2. Specify the range of data records you want to search. Be sure to include in the range the field names at the top of the range and portions of the records that may be off-screen.
3. To specify more than one database, use a comma (**,**) to separate the input ranges. After you specify all the databases, select **OK**.

Notes

Only one database can be specified as the **I**nput range when you are using **D**ata **Q**uery **D**elete, **D**ata **Q**uery **F**ind, or **D**ata **Q**uery **M**odify.

Multiple databases cannot be specified in the **I**nput range if you are planning to work with data in one single database. This restriction is true only when you use **D**ata **Q**uery **E**xtract **u**nique only, **D**ata **Q**uery **M**odify **E**xtract, or **D**ata **Q**uery **E**xtract.

When you are allowed, you can designate more than one database for the **I**nput range if you separate the table addresses or range names with commas.

Data Query Modify

Purpose

Offers an easy way to edit a group of similar records. Use this command to select a group of records, edit them, and then reinsert the records into the database.

To edit a group of similar records

1. Create the criteria range and enter the conditions for the records that you want to modify.
2. Create the output range.
3. Highlight the **I**nput range.

4. Select Data Query by clicking the mouse or pressing Alt+D+Q from the keyboard.
5. The selected range appears in the Input range text box. If not preselected, select the range now.
6. Specify the Criteria range.
7. Specify the Output range.
8. Select Modify.
9. Select Extract to copy records matching the criteria into the output range.
10. Select Cancel to close the Data Query dialog box.
11. Edit the records in the output range.
12. Select Data Query Modify Replace to replace the original records in the input range with the corresponding modified records in the output range, or select Data Query Modify Insert to append the records to the bottom of the input range.
13. Select Cancel to return to READY mode.

Data Query Output Range

Purpose

Designates an area to copy the results of Data Query Extract or Data Query Modify Extract.

To designate an area

1. Enter the Output range field names. If you want a limited number of extracted records, the number of rows in the Output range should equal the number of extracted rows that you want.
2. Select Data Query Output range by clicking the mouse or pressing Alt+D+Q+O from the keyboard.
3. Select OK.

Notes

Field names are contained in the first row of the **O**utput range. The remaining rows are reserved for the data. The **O**utput range can exist in a current file or in the range name of an external table.

If a field name is excluded, no data is extracted for that field.

Data Query Reset

Clears settings for the input, criteria, and output ranges in the current file.

To clear settings

1. Locate the cell pointer in the file containing the settings you want to reset.
2. Select Data Query Reset by clicking the mouse or pressing **Alt**+**D**+**Q**+**R** from the keyboard.

Data Regression

Purpose

Finds trends in data using multiple linear regression techniques.

To find trends in data

1. Select Data Regression by clicking the mouse or pressing **Alt**+**D**+**R** from the keyboard.
2. Select **X**-range; then specify the range, which may contain up to 75 independent variables. The values must be in adjacent columns.
3. Select **Y**-range and specify a single column of dependent variables. This single column must have the same number of rows as the **X**-range.

4. Use the Output range text box to specify the output range.
5. Select Compute or set to zero.
6. Select **OK** to compute the y-intercept or set it to zero.

Note

The X-range (independent variables), the Y-range (dependent variable), and the Output range (contains the results of the analysis) are all required ranges for Data Regression.

Data Sort

Purpose

Sorts the database in ascending or descending order.

To sort a database

1. Highlight the data range to be sorted. You must include every field (column) in the database, but do not include the field labels at the top of the database or the labels will sort with the data.
2. Select Data Sort by clicking the mouse or pressing Alt+D+S from the keyboard.
3. Either accept or change the range displayed in the Data range text box.
4. Select Primary key to designate the first column to be used to sort. Use Primary key to specify Ascending or Descending sort order.
5. Select Secondary key if you want to sort duplicate entries of the Primary key. Specify Ascending or Descending sort order.
6. Select Extra keys if you want to sort on additional keys.
7. In the Key text box, enter the number of the extra keys, from 1 to 253.

8. In the Key range text box, specify any cell in the column to be the extra key.

9. Select Ascending or Descending order; then select Accept. Repeat this step to select additional keys, and select **OK** when finished.

10. Select **OK**.

Note

Sorting can be done on one or more fields (columns). Do not include blank rows or the data labels at the top of the database when you select the data range. Blank rows sort to the top or bottom of the database, and data labels sort into the body of the database.

Data What-if Table

Purpose

Generates a table showing how formula results vary when the numbers used in the formula are changed.

Reminders

Use Data What-if Table to show how changes in one variable affect the output from one or more formulas using a 1-way table. Use Data What-if Table 2-Way to show how changes in two variables affect the output from one formula. Use Data What-if Table 3-Way to show how changes in three variables affect the output from one formula.

To recalculate the same what-if table, press **F8** (Table) after changing the input values.

To set up a 1-way table

1. Select a location for the Table range.

2. Select a location outside the table range for the input cell and label each location.

3. Use the first row of the table range to enter one or more formulas, making sure that each formula refers to the Input cell.

4. Beginning in the second cell in the first column of the table range, enter the input values 1-2-3 will use in the formulas. Make sure that you leave the top left cell of the table blank.

To set up a 2-way table

1. Select a location for the Table range.
2. Select a location outside the table range for the input cells and label each location.
3. Use the top left cell of the table range to enter the formula. Make sure that the formula refers to both input cells.
4. Begin with the cell under the formula in the first column of the table range and enter the input values associated with Input cell 1.
5. Enter the input values associated with Input cell 2 in the cells to the right of the formula.

To set up a 3-way table

1. Select a location for the Table range.
2. Select a location outside of the table range for the input cells and label each location.
3. Use a cell outside of the table range to enter the formula to be analyzed. Make sure that the formula refers to all three Input cells.
4. Using the first worksheet, in the first column of the table range, enter the values related to Input cell 1. Make sure that you copy these values to all worksheets in the table range.
5. In the first worksheet and the first row of the table range, enter the values related to Input cell 2. Make sure that you copy these values to all worksheets in the table range.
6. In the top left corner cell of the table range, enter one input value for Input cell 3 in each worksheet.

To calculate all types of Data What-if Tables

1. Select Data What-if Table (1-way, 2-way, or 3-way) by clicking the mouse or pressing **Alt+D+T** [**1**, **2**, **3**].
2. Use the **T**able range text box to specify the table range (this is the range that contains all formulas and all input values).
3. Use the Input cell text boxes to specify the input cell(s).
4. For a **3-**Way table, use the **F**ormula cell text box to specify the formula cell location.
5. Select **OK**.

Notes

Only formulas and input values should be included in the table range. Input cells should not be included.

For Input values:

- Input cell 1 is always equal to the input values entered in the first column of the table range.
- Input cell 2 is always equal to the input values entered in the first row of the table range.
- Input cell 3 is always equal to the input values entered in the top left corner of the table range.

Edit Clear

Purpose

Removes selected data and formats permanently from the worksheet without using the Clipboard.

To remove data and formats permanently

1. Select the data to be removed.
2. Select **E**dit Clea**r** or press **Del**.

Edit Clear Special

Purpose

Removes selected attributes of a range without using the Clipboard. Enables you to remove the cell contents, the number format, the style, or a graph within a specified range.

To remove select attributes of a range

1. Select the data range.
2. Select Edit Clear Special by clicking the mouse or pressing **Alt+E+R** from the keyboard.
3. Select the attributes you want to remove.
4. Select **OK**.

Edit Copy

Purpose

Copies selected data from the worksheet to the Clipboard.

To copy data to the Clipboard

1. Select the data to be copied by clicking the mouse or pressing the navigation keys.
2. Select Edit Copy by clicking the mouse or pressing **Alt+E+C** (or **Ctrl+Ins**) from the keyboard.

Notes

To copy large selections of data or all the contents of files, use the **F**ile **C**ombine **F**rom, **F**ile **I**mport **F**rom and **F**ile **E**xtract To commands.

The Clipboard holds the data that is cut until another **E**dit Cu**t** or **E**dit **C**opy is performed. Then this data replaces the old data on the Clipboard.

You also can click the Copy to the Clipboard SmartIcon to perform this command on a specified range.

Edit Cut

Purpose

Moves selected data from the worksheet to the Clipboard.

To move data to the Clipboard

1. Select the data to be moved using the mouse or the navigation keys.
2. Select Edit Cut by clicking the mouse or pressing **Alt+E+T** (or **Shift+Del**) from the keyboard.

Notes

The Clipboard holds the data that is cut until another **E**dit Cu**t** or **E**dit **C**opy is performed. Then this data replaces the old data on the Clipboard.

You also can click the Cut to the Clipboard SmartIcon to perform this command on a specified range.

Edit Find

Purpose

Finds and optionally replaces characters in a specified range.

To find characters in a specified range

1. Specify the range you want to search.
2. Select Edit Find by clicking the mouse or pressing **Alt+E+F** from the keyboard.
3. Specify the characters you want to find in the **S**earch for text box.

4. In the Action field, specify the action you want 1-2-3 to take. Select **F**ind to highlight locations of the characters entered in the search range. Select **R**eplace with to replace the characters entered in the search range.

5. If you selected **R**eplace with, enter the characters to use as replacements for the existing characters.

6. In the **S**earch through field, select **L**abels to search through labels only, **F**ormulas to search through formulas only, or **B**oth to search through formulas and labels.

7. To begin the search, select Find **N**ext.

Note

You can select to replace all the characters without displaying their location, locate the characters but not replace them, or replace the characters and highlight their next occurrence before replacing them.

Edit Link Options Create

Purpose

Creates a DDE link between the current file and a file created in another Windows application.

To create a DDE link

1. Select Edit Link Options Create by clicking the mouse or pressing **Alt+E+O+C** from the keyboard.

2. Change the **L**ink name or accept the default name (for example, LINK1).

3. Select the file format of the transferred data from the Format name list.

4. To specify the **U**pdate mode of the link, select **A**utomatic or **M**anual.

5. Specify the destination range in the R**a**nge text box.

6. Select the application from the list of active Windows applications or type the name of an inactive application in the Application text box.

7. Specify the source file in the Topic name text box.
8. Enter the source item in the Item name text box.
9. Select **OK**.

Edit Link Options Deactivate

Purpose

Makes a DDE link inactive so that the values in the destination range are not updated when the source file changes. The link is not deleted, however.

To make a DDE link inactive

1. Select Edit Link Options by clicking the mouse or pressing **Alt+E+O** from the keyboard.
2. In the Links list, select the link to deactivate. Read the Format information box to make sure that you have selected the correct link.
3. Select **D**eactivate.

Edit Link Options Delete

Purpose

Removes DDE links that were created with the **E**dit **P**aste **L**ink or **E**dit Link **O**ptions **C**reate command.

To remove existing DDE links

1. Select Edit Link Options by clicking the mouse or pressing **Alt+E+O** from the keyboard.
2. In the Links list, select the link to remove.
3. Select **D**elete.

Edit Link Options Edit

Purpose

Changes the Update mode (automatic versus manual) or the source of a DDE link in the current worksheet file.

To change the Update mode or the source of a DDE link

1. Select Edit Link Options by clicking the mouse or pressing Alt+E+O from the keyboard.
2. In the Links list, select the link to edit.
3. Select Edit.
4. To select a different file format for the transferred data, select the format from the Format name list.
5. To change the Update mode of the selected link, select Automatic or Manual.
6. If you need to change the destination range, specify another range in the Range text box.
7. To select a different source application for the link, select an application from the list of active Windows applications or type the name of an inactive application in the Application text box.
8. To change the source file, specify the file in the Topic name text box.
9. To change the source item, type the data item in the Item name text box.
10. Select OK.

Edit Link Options Update

Purpose

Updates manual DDE links to the current worksheet file and reactivates and updates a deactivated link.

To use Edit Link Options Update

Select Edit Link Options Update by clicking the mouse or pressing **Alt+E+O+U** from the keyboard.

Edit Move Cells

Purpose

Moves data to another range in the same worksheet file.

Reminder

The **E**dit **M**ove Cells command leaves the source of the data blank and enters the data in the specified destination area. If the destination area contains data, 1-2-3 overwrites the existing data.

To move data to another range

1. Select the data to be moved.
2. Select Edit Move Cells by clicking the mouse or pressing **Alt+E+M** from the keyboard.
3. Verify that the **F**rom text box contains the specific cell or range you want to move. If it does not, edit the text box.
4. At the **T**o text box, enter the address of the upper left corner of the range to check that the data is to be moved.
5. Select **OK**.

Notes

If you want to move only the formatting associated with the selected range, select the **S**tyles only check box.

You also can click the Select the range to move to SmartIcon to perform this command (after selecting the range to move).

Edit Paste

Purpose

Copies selected data from the Clipboard to the current worksheet.

To paste data from the Clipboard into a worksheet

1. Select the location where you want to paste the data.
2. Select Edit Paste by clicking the mouse or pressing **Alt+E+P** (or **Shift+Ins**) from the keyboard.

Notes

To paste the data into multiple locations, select each location and then select Edit Paste for each location.

You also can click the Paste from the Clipboard SmartIcon to perform this command on a specified range.

Edit Paste Link

Purpose

Uses the link reference on the Clipboard to create a new link from another Windows application to the current worksheet file.

To create a new link from another Windows application

Select the Edit Paste Link by clicking the mouse or using **Alt+E+L** from the keyboard.

Note

The Clipboard must contain data copied from a valid source file in order for the Edit Paste Link option to be available. After you select the option, 1-2-3 creates a new link and updates the link automatically whenever the source file changes.

Edit Undo

Purpose

Enables you to cancel the effect of the most recently executed command or action.

Reminder

By default, Undo is disabled when you start 1-2-3 for Windows. You can enable Undo with the Tools User Setup command.

To cancel the most recent command or action

Select Edit Undo by clicking the mouse or pressing Alt+E+U (or Alt+backspace) from the keyboard.

Notes

You cannot use Undo to reverse the effects of printing, File commands, cell-pointer movement, GoTo, Pane, Calc, or a previous Undo command.

You also can click the Undo last command or action SmartIcon to perform this command

Edit Quick Copy

Purpose

Duplicates data from and to a cell or a range. This command copies the cell contents as well as numeric formats and style formatting (fonts, alignment, borders, color, and shading). Also copies only the style formatting or converts formulas into values.

To duplicate data from a cell or range

1. Select the range to copy.
2. Select Edit Quick Copy by clicking with the mouse or pressing Alt+E+Q from the keyboard.
3. The From text box contains the address of the cells to be copied. If you did not preselect a range, select one now.

4. At the To text box, specify the upper left cell in the area where you want the duplicate data to appear.

5. If desired, turn on the Styles only check box to copy only the formatting (not the cell contents).

6. Select **OK**.

Note

You also can click the Select the range to copy to SmartIcon to perform this command (after selecting the range to copy). To copy styles only, click the Select the range to apply current formats to SmartIcon.

File Administration Network Reserve

Purpose

Controls the reservation status of a file. When more than one person can access a file on a network, controls who is permitted to save changes to the original file name.

To control the reservation status of a file

1. Select File Administration Network Reserve by clicking with the mouse or pressing **Alt**+**F**+**D**+**N** from the keyboard.

2. Select one of the following options:

Get	Gets the file reservation for you after you open or retrieve the file and if no one has changed the file since you opened it.
Release	Releases the file reservation so that others can get the reservation.

Get reservation automatically	When checked, gives the file reservation to the first person to open or retrieve the file. When unchecked, the user must issue the File Administration Network Reserve Get command.

3. Use File Save to save the file with the new reservation setting. (If you released the reservation, you cannot save the file.)

File Administration Paste Table

Purpose

Creates a table of information about all active files or files linked to the current worksheet.

To create a table of information

1. Move the cell pointer to a blank area of the worksheet.
2. Select File Administration Paste Table by clicking with the mouse or pressing **Alt+F+D+P** from the keyboard.
3. Select one of the following options:

Active files	Creates a table of open files.
Linked files	Creates a table of files linked to the active worksheet file.

4. If you did not move the cell pointer to a blank area of the worksheet, select the Range text box and then specify the area where you want the table to appear. You need to specify only the upper left cell of the range.
5. Select **OK**.

File Administration Seal File

Purpose

Prevents a format or reservation setting of a file from being changed.

To protect a file's format or reservation setting from change

1. Select File Administration Seal File by clicking with the mouse or pressing **Alt+F+D+S** from the keyboard.
2. Select one of the following options:

Disable all restrictions	Unseals the active worksheet file and its reservation setting.
File and network reservation status	Seals the active worksheet file file and the reservation setting.
Reservation status only	Seals only the reservation setting for the active worksheet file.

3. Select **OK**.
4. When prompted, enter a password.
5. Next to **V**erify, reenter the password.
6. Select **OK**.

File Administration Update Links

Purpose

Recalculates formulas in all active worksheet files that depend on data in other open worksheet files or files on disk. Also, ensures that the worksheet's formulas are using current data when files are shared among users on a network.

To recalculate formulas

Select File Administration Update Links by clicking with the mouse or pressing **Alt+F+D+U** from the keyboard.

File Close

Purpose

Removes the current worksheet from the screen.

To close the current worksheet

1. Position the cell pointer in the worksheet you want to close.
2. Select File Close by clicking the mouse or pressing **Alt+F+C** from the keyboard.

Notes

You also can press **Ctrl+F4** or double-click the Worksheet Control menu box to close a file.

Closing a file does not automatically save a file. See *File Save* or *File Save As*.

File Combine From

Purpose

Combines values or formulas from a file or worksheet on disk into the current file.

Reminder

File **C**ombine From changes the cell formats in the current file to incorporate those of the incoming data.

To combine values or formulas

1. Position the cell pointer in the top left corner of the range where the data is to be combined.

2. Select File Combine From by clicking the mouse or pressing Alt+F+B from the keyboard.
3. In the File name text box, specify the name of the file on disk that contains the data to be combined.
4. Select one of the following options:

Copy	Copies data specified from a worksheet file on disk to the current file, beginning at the current cell.
Add	Beginning at the current cell, adds numeric data from the worksheet file on disk to values or blank cells in the current file.
Subtract	Beginning at the current cell, subtracts numeric data from the worksheet file on disk from values or blank cells in the current file.

5. Select one of the following options:

Entire File	Uses all cells in the worksheet file and combines them with the current worksheet file.
Range	Combines the values in a specified range from a worksheet file on disk with the values in the current worksheet file.

6. Select OK.

File Exit

Purpose

Ends the 1-2-3 for Windows session.

To end the current session

1. Select File Exit by clicking the mouse or pressing Alt+F+X from the keyboard.

2. If you made any changes to open files without saving them, 1-2-3 asks if you want to save the files before exiting the program. Select **Y**es to save all open files with the current names, **N**o to exit without saving the files, or **C**ancel to abort the **F**ile **E**xit command.

File Extract To

Purpose

Saves to disk a portion of the current worksheet as a separate worksheet.

To save a portion of a worksheet as a separate worksheet

1. Select the range that you want to extract.
2. Select File Extract To by clicking the mouse or pressing **Alt+F+E** from the keyboard.
3. Accept or change the range displayed in the R**a**nge text box.
4. Specify the file to extract data to in the File name text box.
5. Select one of the following options:

Formulas	Extracts formulas as well as data.
Values	Converts formulas into values and extracts the specified data.
Text	Creates an ASCII file.

6. Select **OK**.

File Import From Numbers/Text

Purpose

Brings ASCII text files from disk into a current worksheet file.

Reminders

You can use File Import From to transfer data in two ways. The first method (Text) reads each row of ASCII characters as left-aligned labels in a column; the second method (Numbers) reads into separate cells text enclosed in quotation marks or numbers surrounded by spaces or separated by commas.

To insert ASCII text files into the current worksheet file

1. Move the cell pointer to the upper left corner of the range in which you want to import data.
2. Select File Import From by clicking the mouse or pressing **Alt+F+I** from the keyboard.
3. Select Text or Numbers.
4. Select ASCII File name.
5. Select OK.

File Import From Styles

Purpose

Copies the formats, font set, graphics, and named styles from a 1-2-3, Impress, or Allways format file.

To copy information from a format file

1. Select File Import From Styles by clicking the mouse or pressing **Alt+F+I+S** from the keyboard.
2. In the Files list, select the name of the format file to import from. To display files on a different drive, select the **D**rives field and then the drive letter. To display the files in a different subdirectory, use the **D**irectories field.
3. Select one of the following Import options:

All	Copies all style formats, the font set, graphics, and named styles.
Fonts	Copies the font set.
Graphics	Copies graphics (including charts, annotations, CGM and PIC images).
Named styles	Copies the named styles.

4. Select **OK**.

File New

Purpose

Creates a new blank file on disk and positions a new worksheet on-screen before the current worksheet.

To create a new worksheet

Select File New by clicking the mouse or pressing **Alt+F+N** from the keyboard.

Notes

1-2-3 names the new file and displays it in a second window on top of the first one. You can select another name for the file (see File Save, File Save As). You also can move the window to see both windows at once.

See also *Window Tile*.

File Open

Purpose

Loads the specified worksheet file into memory, making it possible for you to work with several files at one time.

To open a specific worksheet

1. Select File Open by clicking the mouse or pressing **Alt+F+O** from the keyboard.
2. Enter the file name in the File **n**ame text box or use the **F**iles and **D**irectories list boxes and the Dri**v**es drop-down box to Select the file you desire.
3. Select **OK**.

Note

You also can click the Open the existing file SmartIcon to perform this command.

File Page Setup

Purpose

Controls the page layout of the printed spreadsheet. In this dialog box, you can specify a header, footer, margins, borders, compression, options, and orientation.

To set up the page

1. Select File Page Setup by clicking with the mouse or pressing **Alt+F+G**.
2. Change the following options, as necessary.

   The **H**eader and **F**ooter options set the one line of text you want to print at the top or bottom of each printed page.

   The Margins field enables you to set new margins (**T**op, **B**ottom, **L**eft, and **R**ight) for printed output.

The Borders field enables you to specify the **C**olumns and Ro**w**s to print at the left and top of each page and print range. Use borders to repeat column or row headings on each page of a long report so that you don't have to tape the pages together.

The Compression field enables you to shrink or enlarge the font used for the print range. Use this feature when you want to try printing a large range on a single page. The three settings are **A**utomatically fit to page, **M**anually size, and **N**one.

The Options field enables you to specify whether the worksheet frame and grid lines are printed. The two settings are Show wor**k**sheet frame and Show **g**rid lines. You can turn on one or both of these options.

Use the Orientation field to select the command that prints the page horizontally (Lan**d**scape) or vertically (**P**ortrait).

The Default Settings field enables you to save the current page setup as the default; new files then automatically have this page setup. Use the **U**pdate command if you discover that you frequently change the page setup to the same settings. Use R**e**store to replace the current settings with the defaults.

With the Named settings options, you can Retrie**v**e or **S**ave setup library files. Create a library for each group of commonly used page settings.

3. Select **OK**.

Note

Inches and millimeters or centimeters may be specified for margin settings by typing **in**, **mm**, or **cm** after the numeric setting is entered.

File Preview

Purpose

Displays the print range as it will appear when printed.

To display the print range

1. Specify a range to preview.
2. Select File Preview by clicking the mouse or pressing **Alt+F+V** from the keyboard.
3. Either accept the range in the Range text box or specify a new range. You can specify multiple ranges by using an argument separator (a comma or semicolon) after each range.
4. Select **OK**.

Notes

You can display the next page by pressing **PgDn**. Press **PgUp** to display the previous page. Press **Esc** to return to the worksheet.

You also can click the Preview the print range to SmartIcon to perform this command on a specified range.

File Print

Purpose

Prints data according to the specified range, pages, and number of copies.

To print data

1. Specify a range to print.
2. Select File Print.
3. To print a range of pages, rather than all pages, enter the appropriate page numbers in the Pages field.
4. Select Page Setup or Preview to change the layout or preview the print range.
5. Select **OK**.

Notes

You can specify multiple ranges by using an argument separator (a comma or semicolon) after each range.

You also can click the Print a range SmartIcon to perform this command on a specified range.

File Printer Setup

Purpose

Specifies the printer destination and enables you to modify printer settings.

To specify print settings

1. Select File Printer Setup by clicking the mouse or pressing **ALT+F+T** from the keyboard.
2. Use the **P**rinters list box to specify the printer to setup.
3. To change printer settings, select **S**etup. This Setup dialog box enables you to change options specific to the printer (resolution, printer model, paper size, memory, and so on). After you finish changing the printer setup, select **OK** to return to the File Printer Setup dialog box.
4. Select **OK**.

File Save

Purpose

Saves the current worksheet file and settings with the same name.

To save a file

1. Position the cell pointer in the file you want to save.
2. Select File Save by clicking the mouse or pressing **Alt+F+S** from the keyboard.

Note

You also can click the Save the current file SmartIcon to perform this command.

File Save As

Purpose

Stores the current worksheet file with a new name or all open files that were modified. Also enables you to save files with passwords.

To save a current file with a new name

1. Select File Save As by clicking the mouse or pressing Alt+F+A from the keyboard.
2. Either accept the file name displayed or change it in the File name text box.
3. Select OK to save the current worksheets or Save All to save all open worksheets that have been modified.

Note

To use a password to protect the file, select Password protect and enter a password in the Password text box. Then enter the same password in the Verify text box and select OK.

Graph Add To Sheet

Purpose

Adds a graph to the current worksheet.

To add a graph to a worksheet

1. Specify a range where you want to place the graph.
2. Select Graph Add to Sheet by clicking the mouse or pressing Alt+G+A from the keyboard.

3. Select the graph you want to add to the worksheet in the Graph name text box.
4. Either accept or change the range that appears in the Range text box.
5. Select **OK**.

Graph Go To

Purpose

Moves the cell pointer to a specified graph in the worksheet.

To move the cell pointer to a graph

1. Select Graph Go To by clicking the mouse or pressing **Alt+G+G** from the keyboard.
2. Use the Graph name text box to specify the graph to go to. All graphs added to the current worksheet are listed in this box name text.
3. Select **OK**.

Graph Import

Purpose

Adds graphs to the current file that are copied from a PIC or CGM file on disk.

To add graphs to the current file

1. Select the range where you want to import the graph.
2. Select Graph Import by clicking the mouse or pressing **Alt+G+I** from the keyboard.
3. Use the File name text box to enter the name of the file that contains the graph to import.
4. Select the CGM or PIC command button in the File type field.

5. Use the Range text box if you need to change the range displayed.

6. Select **OK**.

Graph Name Delete

Purpose

Deletes named graphs that have not been used.

To delete a named graph

1. Select Graph Name by clicking the mouse or pressing Alt+G+M from the keyboard.

2. Enter the name of the graph in the Graph name text box and select Delete. To delete all named graphs from a worksheet, select the Delete All button.

3. Select **OK**.

Graph Name Paste Table

Purpose

Inserts a list of information about the current file's graphs. This three-column table lists each graph's name, type, and title.

To insert information about graphs

1. Position the cell pointer in the upper left corner where you want to insert the table.

2. Select Graph Name Paste Table by clicking the mouse or pressing **Alt+G+M+P** from the keyboard.

3. Verify the range in the Range text box. (The upper left corner of the table is sufficient.)

4. Select **OK**.

Graph New

Purpose

Uses a specified range of data to create and name a graph.

To create and name a graph

1. Select the range that contains the data you want to graph.
2. Select Graph New by clicking the mouse or pressing **Alt+G+N** from the keyboard.
3. Either accept the default name or specify a name for the graph in the **G**raph name text box.
4. Accept or change the range specified in the R**a**nge text box.
5. Select **OK**. The Graph window menu bar appears at the top of the screen.

Notes

After the graph window is activated, the menu bar displays the Graph window commands. The Graph window commands are included after the **G**raph commands in this command reference.

You also can click the Create a new graph SmartIcon to perform this command.

Graph Refresh

Purpose

Reflects recalculation of data ranges by updating all graphs in the current file.

To update a graph

1. Modify data in the graph range and recalculate the worksheet, if necessary.

2. Select Graph Refresh by clicking the mouse or pressing **Alt+G+F** from the keyboard.

Note

Make certain that the current file contains the graph(s).

Graph Size

Purpose

Permits modification of the range that the graph occupies and resizes the graph to the modified range size.

To modify the size of a graph

1. Highlight a cell in the range that includes the graph.
2. Select Graph Size by clicking the mouse or pressing **Alt+G+S** from the keyboard.
3. In the Range text box, specify the range for the graph.
4. Select **OK**.

Graph View

Purpose

Displays a graph created for the current file in the Graph window.

To display a graph

1. Select Graph View by clicking the mouse or pressing **Alt+G+V** from the keyboard.
2. Enter the graph to display text.
3. Select **OK**.

Help

Purpose

Displays context-sensitive help.

To obtain Help information

1. Select Help by clicking the mouse or pressing **Alt+H** from the keyboard.
2. From the Help pull-down menu, select one of the following options to display Help information.

Index	Displays an index of all available Help topics.
Using Help	Describes how to use the Help feature.
Keyboard	Lists keyboard controls, such as function keys, editing keys, and accelerator keys.
@Functions	Describes how to use the built-in @functions of 1-2-3 for Windows.
Macros	Explains what macros are and how to create and use them.
How Do I?	Accesses an alphabetical index of common tasks.
For Upgraders	Displays information for upgraders from DOS versions of 1-2-3.
About 1-2-3	Displays the 1-2-3 for Windows version number and circular references.

3. Select **F**ile **E**xit to return to the worksheet.

To open a new Help file

1. Select File Open from the Help window menu by clicking the mouse or pressing **Alt+F** from the keyboard.

2. Type the name of the file in the filename text box.

3. Select Open

To print a Help topic

1. Select the desired Help topic.

2. Select File Print Topic from the Help window menu by clicking the mouse or pressing **Alt+F+P**. To abandon the printing, select Cancel.

To copy Help information to the Clipboard

1. Select the desired Help topic.

2. Select Edit Copy from the Help window menu by clicking the mouse or pressing **Alt+E+C** (or **Ctrl+Ins**) from the keyboard.

To insert a bookmark in a Help topic

1. Select the desired Help topic.

2. Select Bookmark Define from the Help window menu by clicking the mouse or pressing **Alt+M** from the keyboard.

3. Accept the default Bookmark name or enter a new Bookmark name.

4. Select **OK**.

To delete a bookmark in a Help topic

1. Select Bookmark Define from the Help window menu by clicking the mouse or pressing **Alt+M+D** from the keyboard.

2. Accept the default Bookmark name or type in a new Bookmark Name name.

3. Select the Delete button.

4. Select **OK**.

To Select a bookmark in a Help topic

1. Select Bookmark from the Help window menu by clicking the mouse or pressing **Alt+M** from the keyboard.

2. Select the bookmark name from the menu by selecting the number assigned to the bookmark name or by pointing to the bookmark name and clicking the mouse.

To back up to the last Help screen

From the Help window, select the Back icon by clicking the mouse or pressing Alt+B from the keyboard.

To browse through the Help topics

From the Help window, select the Browse or <<Browse>> icon by clicking the mouse or pressing Alt+R or Alt+O from the keyboard.

To search for a Help topic

1. From the Help window, select the Search icon by clicking the mouse or pressing Alt+S from the keyboard.
2. Enter the Search For information in the text box.
3. When the correct topic is displayed, select the Search button.
4. Select the desired topic in the Topics Found list box.
5. Select the Go To button to display the desired topic.

Range Annotate

Purpose

Creates graphic drawings in a worksheet range. For example, you can use the Graph window to insert text that you rotated 90 degrees, draw and place a logo, and create arrows that point to important parts of the worksheet.

To create graphic drawings in a worksheet range

1. Highlight the range to annotate.
2. Select Range Annotate by clicking the mouse or pressing Alt+R+A from the keyboard.

3. Select **OK**.
4. Create a drawing in the Graph window. See the Graph window commands for details on graphic drawing and manipulation.
5. Select **F**ile **C**lose after you complete the process.

Range Format

Purpose

Changes the way numbers appear in a range.

Reminder

Range formats take precedence over Wor**k**sheet **G**lobal Settings.

To change the appearance of numbers in a range

1. Select the range to format.
2. Select a **F**ormat from the following menu items:

Fixed	Sets the number of decimal places displayed.
Scientific	Displays large or small numbers, using scientific notation.
Currency	Displays currency symbols and commas.
, (Comma)	Inserts commas to mark thousands and multiples of thousands.
General	Displays values with no special formatting.
+/–	Creates horizontal bar graphs. Each symbol is equal to one whole number. Positive numbers are displayed as plus (+) symbols; negative numbers are displayed as minus (–) symbols.

Percent	Displays a decimal number as a whole number followed by a % sign.
Text	Continues to evaluate formulas as numbers, but displays formulas as text on-screen.
Hidden	Hides contents from the display and does not print them, but still evaluates contents.
Automatic	Formats numbers and dates as they are entered in a cell with General format.
Label	Formats all entries as labels using a label prefix.
1:	31-Dec-90
2:	31-Dec
3:	Dec-90
4:	Long Intl Date
5:	Short Intl Date
6:	11:59:59 AM
7:	11:59 AM
8:	Long Intl Time
9:	Short Intl Time

3. Use the **D**ecimal places text box to enter the number of decimal places (0 through 15) displayed in any numeric format except General.
4. Use the **P**arentheses check box to display numeric values enclosed in parentheses.
5. Accept the range displayed in the R**a**nge text box or specify a new range.
6. Use **R**eset to change the range's present format back to the current global cell format.
7. Select **OK**.

Range Go To

Purpose

Enables you to move the cell pointer to a specified cell or named range in any open worksheet file.

To move the cell pointer

1. Select Range Go To by clicking the mouse or pressing Alt+R+G from the keyboard.
2. Specify the range to go to using the Range text box.
3. Select OK.

Range Justify

Purpose

Modifies a column of labels to fit within a specified width.

To modify a column of labels

1. Highlight the range to be justified.
2. Select Range Justify by clicking the mouse or pressing Alt+R+J from the keyboard.

Note

Using Range Justify in GROUP mode affects the corresponding range in all worksheets in the file. Range Justify changes or invalidates the results of any formulas in the Justify range.

Range Name Create

Purpose

Alters range names by creating, deleting and undefining the existing range name.

To alter a range name

1. Select the cell or range to name.
2. Select Range Name Create by clicking the mouse or pressing **Alt+R+N+C** from the keyboard.
3. Use the **R**ange name text box to enter the name for the range.
4. Select **C**reate to create the range name.
5. Repeat steps 3 and 4 to create additional range names.
6. Select **OK**.

Notes

Instead of cell addresses, use range names to make formulas and macros easy to read and understand.

Use a range name when you enter a function. Instead of entering a function as @SUM(P53..P65), for example, type it as **@SUM(EXPENSES)**.

Use a range name when you respond to a prompt. When the program requests a print range, for example, provide a range name, as in the following example:

`Enter print range:` **JULREPORT**

Range Name Delete

Purpose

Removes a range name but does not delete the data in the range.

To delete one or more range names

1. Select Range Name Delete by clicking the mouse or pressing **Alt+R+N+D** from the keyboard.
2. Use the **R**ange Name text box to specify the range name to be deleted.

3. Select one of the following commands:

Delete All	Deletes all defined range names, leaving the data in the ranges unchanged.
Undefine	Cancels the link between a range name from a range address.
Delete	Used to delete the range name specified in the Range Name text box.

Range Name Label Create

Purpose

Assigns range names to single cells using the contents of cells in the highlighted range.

To assign range names to single cells

1. Select the range containing the labels you want to use as range names.
2. Select Range Name Label Create by clicking the mouse or pressing Alt+R+N+L from the keyboard.
3. Select one of the following directions:

Direction	*Function*
Left	Names cells to the left of the labels.
Right	Names cells to the right of the labels.
Up	Names cells above the labels.
Down	Names cells below the labels.

4. Use the Range text box to enter the name for the range to access in order to use labels contained in that range.
5. Select OK.

Range Name Paste Table

Purpose

Inserts a list of information about the current file's range names. This two-column table lists each range name and the corresponding cell addresses of the range names.

To insert information about current range names

1. Move the cell pointer to a blank area of the worksheet. The table requires two columns and as many rows as there are range names.

2. Select Range Name Paste Table by clicking the mouse or pressing **Alt+R+N+P** from the keyboard.

3. If you didn't preposition the cell pointer in the table's destination range, indicate the starting cell for the table in the R**a**nge text box.

4. Select **OK**.

Range Protect

Purpose

Reinstates the protection of unprotected cells in a range of a globally protected worksheet or worksheets.

To reinstate cell protection

1. Define the range you want to protect.

2. Select Range Protect by clicking the mouse or pressing **Alt+R+P** from the keyboard.

Note

You can change formulas and attributes in protected cells, but you cannot change the actual data.

Range Transpose

Purpose

Copies data from one location to another location and orientation. Formulas are replaced by values.

Reorders columns of data into rows and rows of data into columns.

To copy data from one location to another

1. Select the range to be transposed.
2. Select Range Transpose by clicking the mouse or pressing **Alt+R+T** from the keyboard.
3. Use the **F**rom text box to accept the default range or specify a new range.
4. Use the **T**o text box to specify the range you want to copy.
5. Select **OK**.

Notes

Make sure that the source file is calculated. If `Calc` is displayed at the bottom of the screen, press **F9** to recalculate the worksheet.

Transpose the new data to a clear worksheet area. The transposed data overwrites any existing data.

Range Unprotect

Purpose

Enables you to change cells in a globally protected worksheet.

To unprotect a cell

1. Select the range you want to unprotect.

2. Select Range Unprotect by clicking the mouse or pressing **Alt+R+U** from the keyboard.

Style 1 through Style 8

Purpose

Uses customized named styles to format a range.

To format a range using a style

1. Select the range to format.
2. Select Style 1 through 8 by clicking the mouse or pressing **Alt+S** and selecting the number from the keyboard.
3. Select **OK**.

Style Alignment

Purpose

Aligns labels in a range or across the columns of a range.

To align labels in a range

1. Select the range that contains the labels you want to align.
2. Select Style Alignment by clicking the mouse or pressing **Alt+S+A** from the keyboard.
3. Select one of the following options listed under Align labels:

Left	Positions labels at the left edge of cells.
Center	Centers labels in cells.
Right	Positions labels at the right edge of cells.

4. To align labels across a range of columns, select Align over columns. You can select the Even command button to expand the label to fill the column range.

5. Either accept or change the range displayed in the Range text box.

6. Select **OK**.

Note

You can click the Align left, Center, and Align Right SmartIcons to perform these commands on a specified range.

Style Border

Purpose

Displays horizontal and vertical lines along the edges of cells in a range, draws outlines around cells and ranges, and creates drop shadows around ranges.

To draw borders

1. Select the range to apply the borders to.

2. Select Style Border by clicking the mouse or pressing **Alt+S+B** from the keyboard.

3. Select from the following options to draw borders around each cell in a range:

All edges	Displays outlines around each cell in a range.
Top	Displays a line along the top edge of each cell in a range.
Bottom	Displays a line along the bottom edge of each cell in a range.
Left	Displays a line along the left edge of each cell in a range.
Right	Displays a line along the right edge of each cell in a range.

4. Use the drop-down box located to the right of each option to select a line style (thin, double, or thick).

5. Select **O**utline to display a border around the range as a whole and Select the line style from the drop-down box.

6. Select **D**rop shadow to display a drop shadow below and to the right of the range.

7. Either accept or change the range displayed in the R**a**nge text box.

8. Select **OK**.

Style Color

Purpose

Assigns colors to ranges and displays negative values in red.

To assign colors to ranges

1. Specify the range for which you want to specify color.

2. Select Style Color by clicking the mouse or pressing **Alt**+**S**+**C** from the keyboard.

3. Use the **C**ell contents drop-down box to select a color for the data.

4. Use the **B**ackground drop-down box to select a color for the background.

5. To display negative values in red, select the **N**egative values in red check box.

6. Either accept or change the range displayed in the R**a**nge text box.

7. Select **OK**.

Style Font

Purpose

Specifies the default font set for a worksheet file, specifies fonts and text attributes for ranges, and saves font libraries in files on disk.

To assign a font to a range

1. Select the range to be changed.
2. Select Style Font by clicking the mouse or pressing Alt+S+F from the keyboard.
3. Use the Fonts list box to select the font you want to use.
4. Use the Bold, Italics, or Underline check box to add these attributes to the range.
5. Either accept or change the range displayed in the Range text box.
6. Select **OK**.

To replace a font in the current set

1. Select Style Font Replace by clicking with the mouse or pressing Alt+S+F+R from the keyboard.
2. In the Current fonts list, select the font to replace.
3. In the Available fonts list, select a new typeface.
4. In the Size list, select a point size.
5. Select Replace (or select **OK** if you have no more fonts to replace).
6. Repeat steps 2 through 5 for each font to be replaced.
7. Select **OK**.

Note

You can also click the Bold, Italics, and Underline SmartIcons to assign these styles to a specified range.

Style Name

Purpose

Creates a named style from the format of a cell.

To create a named style

1. Select the cell with the format you want to use for a named style.
2. Select Style Name by clicking the mouse or pressing **Alt+S+N** from the keyboard.
3. Select an option from **1** through **8** to designate the named style.
4. Type a name of up to six characters to be used as the style name.
5. Enter up to 36 characters to describe the named style.
6. Accept the range in the R**a**nge text box or specify a new one.
7. Select **OK**.

Notes

After you enter the named style, it appears in the **S**tyle pull-down menu next to its corresponding number.

If you highlight the corresponding named-style number, the description appears in the title bar.

Style Shading

Purpose

Adds light, dark, or solid shading to a specified range.

To shade a range

1. Specify the range where you want to add (or remove shading.
2. Select Style Shading by clicking the mouse or pressing **Alt+S+S** from the keyboard.

3. Select one of the following options:

Light	Adds light shading to a range.
Dark	Adds dark shading to a range.
Solid	Adds solid shading to a range.
Clear	Removes shading from a range.

4. Accept or change the range that appears in the Range text box.

5. Select **OK**.

Tools Add-in

Purpose

Enables you to start add-ins or remove add-ins from memory.

To start an add-in

1. Select Tools Add-in by clicking the mouse or pressing **Alt+T+A** from the keyboard.

2. Select Load and specify the name of the add-in to read into memory in the File name text box.

3. Select **OK**.

Note

Add-ins can be applications, functions, or macro commands.

Tools Backsolver

Purpose

Changes a variable that affects the results of a formula and calculates that formula to achieve a desired value.

To use Tools Backsolver

1. Type the formula in a cell that Backsolver will solve.
2. Determine the desired result of the formula.
3. Determine which variable will be changed.
4. Select Tools Backsolver by clicking the mouse or pressing **Alt+T+B** from the keyboard.
5. Use the **M**ake cell text box to specify the address of the cell that contains the formula.
6. Use the **E**qual to value text box to enter the desired value of the formula.
7. Use the **B**y changing cell text box to specify the address of the variable to change.
8. Select **S**olve.

Tools Macro Debug

Purpose

Begins STEP and TRACE modes used to debug a macro.

To debug a macro

1. Select Tools Macro Debug by clicking the mouse or pressing **Alt+T+M** from the keyboard.
2. Select the **S**ingle step and **T**race text boxes.
3. Select **OK**.
4. Start the macro.
5. Press any key to execute one instruction at a time until you encounter the instruction causing the error.

Note

The Step indicator and the Macro Trace window remain on-screen until you turn off the check boxes in the Tools Macro Debug dialog box.

Tools Macro Run

Purpose

Selects and runs a macro.

To select and run a macro

1. Select Tools Macro Run by clicking the mouse or pressing **Alt+T+M+R** from the keyboard.
2. Enter the name of the macro in the Macro name text box.
3. Select **OK**.

Tools Macro Show Transcript

Purpose

Displays the contents of the Transcript window. The Transcript window is a temporary storage area that contains the last 512 characters you typed. By displaying the transcript, you can copy selected keystrokes into the worksheet to use in a macro. You also can run the macro directly from the Transcript window. The options on the menu that results when you activate the Transcript window are covered in subsequent sections.

To display to the contents of the Transcript window

1. Select Tools Macro Show Transcript by clicking the mouse or pressing **Alt+T+M+S** from the keyboard.
2. Click this window to make it active or press **Ctrl+F6**.
3. If desired, move or resize the window.
4. To take keystrokes from the Transcript window to the worksheet, highlight the desired keystrokes; then use Edit Cut and Edit Paste.
5. After you no longer need the Transcript window, select File Close while the Transcript window is active.

Tools SmartIcons

Purpose

Positions, hides, or customizes the icon palette.

To customize the icon palette

1. Select Tools SmartIcons by clicking the mouse or pressing **Alt+T+I** from the keyboard.
2. Select one of the following palette positions:

Left	Positions the icon palette vertically on the left side of the 1-2-3 window.
Right	Positions the icon palette vertically on the right side of the 1-2-3 window.
Top	Positions the icon palette horizontally at the top of the 1-2-3 window. This is the default setting for 1-2-3 for Windows.
Bottom	Positions the icon palette horizontally at the bottom of the 1-2-3 window.
Floating	Enables the icon palette to be moved to any position on the screen and to be resized to display more or fewer icons.

3. To suppress the display of the icon palette, select the **H**ide palette check box.
4. Select **OK**.

Tools SmartIcons Customize

Purpose

Selects which SmartIcons appear on the displayed icon palette and enables you to create custom SmartIcons.

To add a standard icon to the current icon palette

1. Select Tools SmartIcons Customize by clicking the mouse or pressing Alt+T+I+C from the keyboard.
2. In the Standard icons area, click the SmartIcon you want to add; you may need to use the scroll bar to display additional icons.
3. To make sure that you are adding the correct icons, read the description at the bottom of the dialog box.
4. Select the Add button.
5. Repeat steps 2 through 4 for each SmartIcon you want to add.
6. Select OK.

To remove an icon from the current icon palette

1. Select Tools SmartIcons Customize by clicking the mouse or pressing Alt+T+I+C from the keyboard.
2. In the current icon palette, click the SmartIcon you want to remove; you may need to use the scroll bar to display additional icons.
3. To make sure that you are deleting the correct icon, read the description at the bottom of the dialog box.
4. Select the Remove button.
5. Repeat steps 2 through 4 for each SmartIcon you want to remove.
6. Select OK.

To create a custom SmartIcon

1. Create a bit-map image that illustrates the SmartIcon's task. Save the file in the \123W\SHEETICO or \123W\GRAPHICO directory (depending on whether the icon applies to the Worksheet or Graph window).
2. Create the macro you want to assign to the icon.
3. Highlight the range that contains the macro. (You must highlight all cells—not just the first one.)

4. Select Tools SmartIcons Customize by clicking the mouse or pressing **Alt+T+I+C** from the keyboard. The new bit-map image automatically appears in the Custom icons box.
5. Click the new icon in the Custom icons box.
6. Select **A**ssign macro.
7. Select **G**et macro and the macro keystrokes appear in the Macro box.
8. Select **OK**.

To add a custom SmartIcon to the icon palette

1. In the Custom icons section of the Tools SmartIcons Customize dialog box, click the SmartIcon you want to add.
2. Select the **A**dd button.
3. Select **OK**.

Tools Solver

Purpose

Solves what-if problems by changing values in more than one cell to meet multiple goals or constraints.

To change the value in more than one cell

1. Enter the formulas and constraints that describe the problem to solve in the worksheet.
2. Select Tools Solver by clicking the mouse or pressing **Alt+T+S** from the keyboard.
3. Use the **A**djustable cells text box to specify the cells that Solver adjusts to solve the problem.
4. Use the **C**onstraint cells text box to specify the cells that contain the logical formulas.
5. Use the **O**ptimal cell text box if you want to specify the optimal cell.

6. If you want to limit the number of possible answers, select Options, enter a number next to Number of answers, and select OK.
7. Select Solve.
8. Select Next to continue to display additional answers.
9. Select Cancel to leave the Solver and return to the worksheet.

Note

The Solver displays the Solver Answer dialog box and places the first answer in the worksheet. The Solver produces a progress report showing how many answers it has found in the Solver Answer dialog box.

Tools User Setup

Purpose

Modifies settings that affect the display and behavior of 1-2-3 for Windows.

To modify 1-2-3 for Windows settings

1. Select Tools User Setup by clicking the mouse or pressing Alt+T+U from the keyboard.
2. Select or deselect the check box of one or more of the following options:

Beep on error	Sets the computer's bell to sound when errors occur or when a {BEEP} command occurs in a macro.
Enable Edit Undo	Enables or disables Edit Undo.
Run autoexecute macros	Signals 1-2-3 to run autoexecute macros.

3. Select the Worksheet directory text box to enter the default directory.

4. Select one of the following options under Clock display to control the date and time in the status line:

Standard	Displays the date in DD-MMM-YY format and the time in HH:MM format.
International	Displays the date in Long International format and the time in Short International format.
None	Removes the date and time from the status line.

5. Select International to set the punctuation for numbers, the argument separators for @functions and macro commands, the currency symbol and location, the international date and time formats, and the display of negative numbers in Comma and Currency formats.

6. Select Recalculation to designate when and in what order 1-2-3 will recalculate formulas and how many recalculation passes (iterations) will be performed each time recalculation occurs in active files.

7. Select Update if you want to store the new default settings and replace the current defaults.

8. Select **OK**.

Note

If Update is not selected, the changes made only affect the current session.

Window 1 through n

Purpose

Selects a window to make active. Capable of listing up to nine Worksheet, Graph, and Transcript windows that are open in the 1-2-3 window and designates the active window by displaying a check mark next to it.

To make a window active

Select Window 1 through *n* by clicking the mouse or pressing **Alt**+**W**+*n* from the keyboard.

Note

You can make a window active by positioning the mouse pointer in the desired window and clicking the window. You also can press **Ctrl**+**PgUp** or **Ctrl**+**PgDn** to relocate the cell pointer to the desired window.

Window Cascade

Purpose

Arranges and sizes all open Worksheet, Graph, and Transcript windows in the 1-2-3 window so that they overlap one another.

To arrange and size open windows

Select Window Cascade by clicking the mouse or pressing **Alt**+**W**+**C** from the keyboard.

Note

The active window appears first, and all other windows appear behind and above the windows in front, leaving only title bars visible.

Window Display Options

Purpose

Regulates settings for colors, grid lines, and the display of the worksheet frame for the current worksheet.

To regulate worksheet attributes

1. Select Window Display Options by clicking the mouse or pressing **Alt**+**W**+**D** from the keyboard.

2. Select the following options to modify the display:

Colors	Assigns colors to the worksheet frame, cell background, cell contents, negative values, drop shadows, grid lines, range borders, selected ranges and unprotected cells.
Options	Specifies whether the worksheet appears with page breaks, in draft or graphic display, in monochrome or color display, and with grid lines.
Frame	Changes the style of the worksheet frame.
Zoom	Changes the display size of worksheet cells.
Palette	Sets the colors for the worksheet display.

3. Select **U**pdate to store the new default settings, or **R**estore to replace the new settings with the default settings.

4. Select **OK**.

Window More Windows

Purpose

Lists all open Worksheet, Graph, and Transcript windows.

To list open windows

1. Select Window More Windows by clicking the mouse or pressing **Alt+W+M** from the keyboard.

2. Use the Select Window dialog box to specify a window.

3. Select **OK**.

Reminder

When more than nine windows are open in 1-2-3, the Window More Windows menu item will be available on the Window pull-down menu.

Window Split

Purpose

Displays a Worksheet window divided horizontally or vertically; capable of displaying three contiguous worksheets from the same worksheet file in perspective view.

To split a window

1. Select Window Split by clicking the mouse or pressing Alt+W+S from the keyboard.
2. Select Perspective, Horizontal, Vertical, or Clear.
3. Select Synchronize from the Window Split dialog box to scroll worksheets together (the default setting).
4. Select OK.

Note

You also can click the Perspective View SmartIcon to view three worksheets from a file at the same time. While in perspective view, you can select the Go to the next worksheet and Go to the previous worksheet SmartIcons to move the cell pointer between worksheets.

Window Tile

Purpose

Sizes all open Worksheet, Graph, and Transcript windows, placing them side-by-side in the 1-2-3 window.

To size all open windows

Select Window Tile by clicking the mouse or pressing **Alt+W+T** from the keyboard.

Note

The active window displays in the top left corner and all other open windows display as tiles.

Worksheet Column Width

Purpose

Adjusts the column width of one or more columns. You can use this option to reset columns to the global column width.

To set the column width from the keyboard

1. Designate the range of columns whose width is going to be set or reset.
2. Select Worksheet Column Width by clicking the mouse or pressing **Alt+K+C** from the keyboard.
3. Select **S**et width to and use the characters text box to decrease or increase the number for the column width by entering a value from 1 to 240.
4. You can select **R**eset to global to change the column-width of selected columns to the default.
5. Select **OK**.

To set the column width with the mouse

With 1-2-3 in READY mode, move the mouse pointer to the border of the column to the right or left of the column letter and drag the mouse pointer to the right until the column is the desired width.

Notes

Font sizes affect the number of characters you can display across a column. The default column width is 9 and the default font is set to Arial MT 10 point.

*** (asterisks) appear when a column is too narrow to display an entire value as it is formatted.

Labels that are longer than the cell they occupy display across the cell into the next blank cell. If the cell is not blank, only part of the label that fits into the cell will display.

Worksheet Delete

Purpose

Deletes one or more columns, rows, or worksheets from the current file.

To delete parts of worksheets from the current file

1. Highlight a range that includes the columns, rows, or worksheets that you want to delete.
2. Select Worksheet Delete by clicking the mouse or pressing Alt+K+D from the keyboard.
3. Select Column, Row, or Sheet.
4. Select OK.

Worksheet Global Settings

Purpose

Adjusts the default settings in the active worksheet. In the Worksheet Global Settings dialog box, you can control the default column width, format, label alignment, and zero display. You can also turn on Group mode and the protection feature.

To adjust the default settings

1. Select Worksheet Global Settings by clicking with the mouse or pressing Alt+K+G from the keyboard.
2. Select the desired settings from the Worksheet Global Settings dialog box as follows:

The Zero display field contains options that determine how, and if, zeros are displayed in the worksheet. The three settings are Display **z**eros, Leave zeros **b**lank, and **U**se label.

The Column **w**idth text box sets the default column width for the entire worksheet.

The Align labels field contains options that enable you to determine the default alignment (**L**eft, **R**ight, or **C**enter) for labels.

The **G**roup mode check box enables you to make formatting changes that affect all worksheets in the file.

The **P**rotection check box activates the protection feature that prevents certain cells from being changed.

3. Select **OK**.

Worksheet Global Settings Format

Purpose

Establishes the default format for numbers in the current worksheet. Values, for example, can be displayed with a fixed number of decimal places, as currency, with commas, in scientific notation, or as dates and times.

To set the default format for numbers

1. Select Worksheet Global Settings Format by clicking with the mouse or pressing **Alt+K+G+F** from the keyboard.
2. Select a menu item from the following options:

Fixed	Fixes the number of decimal places.
Scientific	Displays numbers in scientific notation.

Currency	Displays numbers with currency symbols and commas.
, Comma	Inserts commas as thousands separators.
General	Displays values with up to 10 decimals or in scientific notation.
+/–	Creates horizontal bar graphs or time-duration graphs on computers that do not have graphics. Each symbol equals one whole number. Positive numbers display as plus (+) signs; negative numbers, as minus (–) signs; and numbers between –1 and 1, as periods.
Percent	Displays a decimal number as a whole number followed by a percent (%) sign.
Text	Displays formulas as text, but continues to evaluate formulas as numbers.
Hidden	Hides contents from the display and printing, but still evaluates contents.
Automatic	Formats numbers and dates automatically when they are entered in a cell that has the General format.
Label	Formats numeric data and entries as labels by using a label prefix.
1:	31-Dec-90
2:	31-Dec
3:	Dec-90
4:	Long Intl Date
5:	Short Intl Date

6:	11:59:59 AM
7:	11:59 AM
8:	Long Intl Time
9:	Short Intl Time

3. To enclose all numbers in parentheses, turn on the Parentheses check box.
4. If applicable, enter a number in the Decimal places text box.
5. Select OK to close the Worksheet Global Settings Format dialog box.
6. Select OK to close the Global Settings dialog box.

Worksheet Hide

Purpose

Hides columns or worksheets.

To hide a column or worksheet

1. Highlight one cell in each column or worksheet you want to hide.
2. Select Worksheet Hide by clicking the mouse or pressing Alt+K+H from the keyboard.
3. Select Column or Sheet.
4. Use the Range text box to confirm or change the range.
5. Select OK.

Worksheet Insert

Purpose

Inserts one or more blank columns, rows, or worksheets into the current file.

To insert a column or a row

1. Designate a range that contains at least one cell at the location of the columns or rows you want to insert.
2. Select Worksheet Insert by clicking the mouse or pressing Alt+K+I from the keyboard.
3. Select Row or Column.
4. Use the Range text box to confirm or change the range displayed.
5. Select OK.

To insert a worksheet

1. Locate the cell pointer in the worksheet in front or behind the worksheet where you want the new worksheet(s) to display.
2. Select Worksheet Insert by clicking the mouse or pressing Alt+K+I from the keyboard.
3. Select Sheet.
4. Designate Before or After to define where you want the new worksheet(s) to display.
5. Use the Quantity text box to enter the number of worksheets to insert.
6. Use the Range text box to confirm or change the range displayed.
7. Select OK.

Worksheet Page Break

Purpose

Manually inserts horizontal and vertical page breaks in printed worksheets.

To insert page breaks manually

1. Move the cell pointer in the column you want to be the leftmost column of the new page, in the row you want to be the top row of the new page, or at the

intersection of the row and the column that will be the topmost row and the leftmost column in the new page.

2. Select Worksheet Page Break by clicking the mouse or pressing **Alt+K+P** from the keyboard.
3. Select one of the following options:

Horizontal	Inserts a horizontal page break, using the row with the selected cell as the top row of the new page.
Vertical	Inserts a vertical page break, using the column with the selected cell as the leftmost column of the new page.
Both	Inserts a page break, using the selected cell as the cell that marks the top row and the leftmost column of the new page.
Clear	Removes the manual page break associated with the selected cell.

4. Select **OK**.

Notes

1-2-3 displays a dashed line along the left of the column for a vertical page break, along the top of the row for a horizontal page break, or along the left of the column and the top of the row for a page break in both directions. These lines are only displayed when you select the Page breaks option from the Window Display Options menu.

Page lengths set through File Print or File Page Setup are overridden by a manual page break set with Worksheet Page Break.

Worksheet Row Height

Purpose

Sets the height of one or more rows in a worksheet. You also may use this option to reset rows to the default row height for the current global font.

To adjust the height of a row

1. Select the range of rows to set the height.
2. Select Worksheet Row Height by clicking the mouse or pressing **Alt+W+R** from the keyboard.
3. Select **S**et height to and enter a height for the row (in points).
4. Use the R**a**nge text box to confirm or change the range displayed.
5. You can select **R**eset height to change the row height of selected rows to the default.
6. Select **OK**.

Worksheet Titles

Purpose

Displays row or column headings that might otherwise be scrolled off the screen.

To display row or column headings

1. If you want to freeze both rows and columns, position the cell pointer in the cell that is below the rows and to the right of the columns you want to freeze.
2. Select Worksheet Titles by clicking the mouse or pressing **Alt+K+T** from the keyboard.

3. Select one of the following options:

Horizontal	Freezes the rows above the cell pointer.
Vertical	Freezes the columns to the left of the cell pointer.
Both	Freezes the rows above and columns to the left of the cell pointer.
Clear	Unfreezes all title rows and columns.

4. Select OK.

Worksheet Unhide

Purpose

Redisplays columns or worksheets that were hidden with Worksheet Hide.

To redisplay hidden columns or worksheets

1. Designate the range of columns or worksheets you want to display.
2. Select Worksheet Unhide by clicking the mouse or pressing Alt+K+U from the keyboard.
3. Select Column or Sheet.
4. Use the Range text box to confirm or change the range.
5. Select OK.

GRAPH WINDOW COMMAND REFERENCE

This Command Reference includes all the 1-2-3 for Windows commands that you can access from the Graph Window. You access the Graph Window by selecting Graph New or Graph View from the Main menu.

Chart Axis

Purpose

Modifies the scale along the x- and y-axes. You can manually change the scale's upper and lower limits, format the numbers, and add a title to the axes.

To modify the scale along x- and y-axes

1. In the Graph window, select Chart Axis by clicking the mouse or pressing Alt+C+A from the keyboard.
2. Select X, Y, or 2nd Y.
3. To set a unique scale, select Manual in the Scale axis field and enter values in the Lower and Upper text boxes. To have 1-2-3 for Windows calculate the scale, select Automatic.
4. To set the order of magnitude (factor of 10) for numbers on the scale, select Manual in the Axis units field and enter a value (between -95 and 95) in the Exponent text box. To have 1-2-3 calculate a scaling factor, select Automatic.
5. For the kinds of scale, select Standard, Logarithmic, or Percentage.
6. To select the numeric format, select Format. After specifying the Format and Decimal places, select OK.

7. Select Options and specify the following options, if desired:

Axis title	A label that describes the data on the axis.
Automatic	Automatically creates the axis-unit name based on the order of magnitude used for the scale numbers.
Manual	Uses the axis-unit name (such as Thousands or Millions) that you specify.
Display label every *n* ticks	Specifies the intervals at which the x-axis scale tick marks are to appear. (This option is available only in the Chart Axis X Options dialog box.)

8. Select OK to close the Options dialog box.
9. Select OK to close the Chart Axis dialog box.

Chart Borders/Grids

Purpose

Turns on and off the borders that surround the chart and the grid lines extending from the axis tick marks.

To turn borders off and on

1. In the Graph window, select Chart Borders/Grids by clicking the mouse or pressing Alt+C+B from the keyboard.
2. To turn borders on or off, select Left, Right, Top, and Bottom—or a combination of a vertical and a horizontal border.
3. To turn grid lines on or off, select X-axis, Y-axis, and/or 2nd Y-axis.
4. Select OK.

Chart Clear

Purpose

Resets graph ranges and settings to the defaults. You can cancel some or all of a graph's settings.

To reset ranges and settings to defaults

1. In the Graph window, select Chart Clear by clicking the mouse or pressing **Alt+C+C** from the keyboard.
2. To clear the X-range and all six data ranges, turn on the All (X, A-F) check box. To clear individual ranges, select **X**, **A**, **B**, **C**, **D**, **E**, and/or **F**. To clear the ranges and all the settings on the Chart menu, turn on the Entire chart check box. To leave the ranges intact but clear the chart's other settings, turn on the Chart settings check box.
3. Select **OK**.

Chart Data Labels

Purpose

Places labels or values next to data points on a graph. Data labels indicate the exact value or a brief description of each data point on the graph.

To place labels or values on a graph

1. In the Graph window, select Chart Data Labels by clicking the mouse or pressing **Alt+C+D** from the keyboard.
2. Next to each text box (**A** through **F**) specify the data-label range, and Select a position (Above, Center, Below, Left, or Right) from the drop-down list.
3. Select **OK**.

Chart Data Labels Group Range

Purpose

Specifies all the data-label ranges at one time. The labels or values are placed next to the corresponding data points on a graph.

To specify data-label ranges

1. In the Graph window, select Chart Data Labels Group Range by clicking the mouse or pressing **Alt+C+D+G** from the keyboard.
2. Select **C**olumnwise if the data-label ranges are in columns; select **R**owwise if the data-label ranges are in rows.
3. Select the R**a**nge text box, and highlight or enter the address of the range of data labels.
4. Select Label position and select a position (Above, Center, Below, Left, or Right) from the drop-down list.
5. Select **OK**. The appropriate ranges fill into the Chart Data Labels dialog box.
6. Select **OK**.

Chart Headings

Purpose

Adds titles and footnotes to a graph.

To add titles and footnotes to a graph

1. In the Graph window, select Chart Headings by clicking the mouse or pressing **Alt+C+H** from the keyboard.
2. Select the **T**itle text box and specify the primary title of the graph.

3. Select the Subtitle text box and specify the second title.
4. Select the Note text box and specify the first footnote.
5. Select the 2nd note text box and specify the second footnote.
6. Select **OK**.

Chart Legend

Purpose

Creates legend labels that identify the data ranges on a graph.

To create legend labels

1. In the Graph window, select Chart Legend by clicking the mouse or pressing Alt+C+L from the keyboard.
2. To assign legend labels to one data range at a time, select the appropriate text box (**A** through **F**); then enter the legend label for each data range. You can type a label, such as **Region 1**, or a backslash followed by the address of a cell that contains the label, such as **\B3**.
3. To assign labels to all the data ranges in one step, select Group Range. Enter the address of the range that contains the legend labels in the Range text box and select **OK**.
4. Select **OK**.

Chart Options Advanced Styles

Purpose

Assigns a color or hatching pattern to each data point.

To assign colors or patterns to data points

1. In the Worksheet window, enter the hatch and/or color codes for each data range.
2. In the Graph window, select Chart Options Advanced Styles by clicking the mouse or pressing **Alt+C+O+A** from the keyboard.
3. For each data range (**A** through **F**) in the first column of text boxes, specify the color range.
4. For each data range (**A** through **F**) in the second column of text boxes, specify the hatch range.
5. Select **OK**.

Chart Options Colors

Purpose

Assigns different colors to text and data ranges.

To assign colors to text and ranges

1. In the Graph window, select Chart Options Colors by clicking the mouse or pressing **Alt+C+O+C** from the keyboard.
2. Select **C**hart title and choose a color from the drop-down list.
3. Select **S**ubtitle, axis titles, legend. Choose a color from the drop-down list.
4. Select **L**abels, notes, name of units. Choose a color from the drop-down list.
5. For each data range color you want to change, select the appropriate letter (**A** through **F**) and choose a color from the drop-down list.
6. Select **OK**.

Chart Options Fonts

Purpose

Selects different fonts for the headings and labels on a chart.

To change fonts in charts

1. In the Graph window, select Chart Options Fonts by clicking the mouse or pressing **Alt+C+O+F** from the keyboard.
2. Select **C**hart title and choose a font from the drop-down list.
3. Select **S**ubtitle, axis titles, legend. Choose a font from the drop-down list.
4. Select **L**abels, notes, name of units. Choose a font from the drop-down list.
5. Select **OK**.

Chart Options Hatches

Purpose

Designates the kind of cross-hatching patterns that fill each data range in a chart.

To select patterns for data ranges

1. In the Graph window, select Chart Options Hatches by clicking the mouse or pressing **Alt+C+O+H** from the keyboard.
2. For each data-range hatching pattern you want to change, select the appropriate letter (**A** through **F**) and choose a pattern from the drop-down list.
3. Select **OK**.

Chart Options Lines

Purpose

Formats lines in charts that contain lines (line, mixed, HLCO, and XY charts).

You can format lines three ways. The Connectors option connects data points with a line. The Symbols option places a symbol at each data point. The Area fill option fills the space between data ranges or between a range and the X-axis.

To format lines in charts

1. In the Graph window, select Chart Options Lines by clicking the mouse or pressing **Alt**+**C**+**O**+**L** from the keyboard.
2. For each data range you want to change, select the appropriate letter (**A** through **F**) and turn on or off Connectors, Symbols, and Area fill.
3. Select **OK**.

Chart Ranges

Purpose

Specifies the worksheet ranges to be graphed.

To specify ranges to be graphed

1. Use the **W**indow **T**ile command to view the Graph and Worksheet windows.
2. In the Graph window, select Chart Ranges by clicking the mouse or pressing **Alt**+**C**+**R** from the keyboard. The dialog box displays the current graph ranges.
3. To change the X-range, select the **X** data range text box and highlight or enter the address of the range

that contains labels for the x-axis (in a pie graph, the labels of the pie slices; in an XY graph, the contents that determine the x-axis numeric scale).

4. To change the first data range, select the A text box and highlight or enter the address of the range.
5. If the graph contains additional data ranges, select the appropriate text box (B, C, D, E, F) and specify the range.
6. To assign a data range to the second y-axis, turn on the appropriate 2nd Y check box.
7. Select OK.

Chart Ranges Group Range

Purpose

Specifies all the graph ranges (X-axis and A through F) at one time. This command is similar to Graph New, except Chart Ranges Group Range accepts data in a columnwise or rowwise orientation.

To specify all ranges

1. In the Graph window, select Chart Ranges Group Range by clicking the mouse or pressing Alt+C+R+G from the keyboard.
2. Select Columnwise if the data ranges are in columns; select Rowwise if the data ranges are in rows.
3. Select the Range text box and highlight or enter the address of the range to be graphed.
4. Select OK. The appropriate ranges are now filled into the Chart Ranges dialog box.
5. To assign a data range to the second y-axis, turn on the appropriate 2nd Y check box.
6. Select OK.

Chart Type

Purpose

Specifies the style of graph you want to use in the current window. Eleven chart types are available in either a vertical or horizontal orientation. One or more styles exist within each basic type.

To specify a style of graph

1. In the Graph window, select Chart Type by clicking the mouse or pressing Alt+C+T from the keyboard.
2. Select the type of graph you want: Line, Area, Bar, Pie, XY, HLCO, Mixed, 3D Line, 3D Area, 3D Bar, or 3D Pie.
3. If more than one style is available, click the appropriate icon in the style gallery.
4. Select the orientation: Vertical or Horizontal.
5. If desired, turn on Include table of values.
6. Select **OK**.

Note

Most available graph types can be selected by clicking on one of the SmartIcons in the Graph window icon palette.

Draw Arrow

Purpose

Creates an arrow in the Graph window.

To create an arrow in the Graph window

1. In the Graph window, select Draw Arrow by clicking the mouse or pressing Alt+D+A from the keyboard.
2. Use the mouse or the arrow keys to specify the location of the first point on the arrow.

3. Press **Enter** or click the mouse button.
4. Use the mouse or the arrow keys to draw the arrow.
5. Press **Enter** or double-click to complete drawing the arrow.

Note

You also can draw an arrow by clicking the Add an arrow icon in the icon palette.

Draw Ellipse

Purpose

Adds a circle or an oval shape to the Graph window.

To add circles or ovals to the Graph window

1. In the Graph window, select Draw Ellipse by clicking the mouse or pressing **Alt+D+E** from the keyboard.
2. Use the mouse or arrow keys to specify the location of one corner of the ellipse.
3. Press **Enter** or click and hold the mouse button.
4. Use the arrow keys or drag the mouse to stretch the ellipse to the desired size.
5. Press **Enter** or release the mouse button.

Note

You also can draw an ellipse by clicking the Add an ellipse icon in the icon palette.

Draw Freehand

Purpose

Draws a free-form shape in the Graph window. This command is similar to using an Etch-a-Sketch.

To draw a free-form shape in the Graph window

1. In the Graph window, select Draw Freehand by clicking the mouse or pressing **Alt+D+F** from the keyboard.
2. Use the mouse or the arrow keys to specify the beginning of the shape.
3. Press **Enter** or click and hold the mouse button.
4. Use the mouse or the arrow keys to draw the shape.
5. Press **Enter** or release the mouse button to finish the object.

Note

You also can draw freehand by clicking the Draw freehand icon in the icon palette.

Draw Line

Purpose

Creates a line, or several connected lines, in the Graph window.

To create a line in the Graph window

1. In the Graph window, select Draw Line by clicking the mouse or pressing **Alt+D+L** from the keyboard.
2. Use the mouse or the arrow keys to specify the beginning of the line.
3. Press **Enter** or click the mouse button.
4. Use the mouse or the arrow keys to draw the line.
5. To draw additional line segments connected to the first, press the **space bar** or click once.
6. Press **Enter** or double-click to finish the line.

Note

You also can draw a line by clicking the Add a line icon in the icon palette.

Draw Polygon

Purpose

Creates a multi-sided object (a polygon) in the Graph window.

To create a polygon in the Graph window

1. In the Graph window, select Draw Polygon by clicking the mouse or pressing **Alt+D+P** from the keyboard.
2. Use the mouse or the arrow keys to specify the beginning of the first line segment.
3. Press **Enter** or click the mouse button.
4. Use the mouse or the arrow keys to draw the first line of the polygon.
5. Press the **space bar** or click once.
6. Continue drawing sides of the polygon, finishing each side by pressing the **space bar** or clicking once.
7. Press **Enter** or double-click to finish the polygon.

Note

You also can draw a polygon by clicking the Add a polygon icon in the icon palette.

Draw Rectangle

Purpose

Adds a square or rectangle to the Graph window.

To add a square or rectangle to the Graph window

1. In the Graph window, select Draw Rectangle by clicking the mouse or pressing **Alt+D+R** from the keyboard.
2. Use the mouse or arrow keys to specify the location of one corner of the rectangle.

3. Press **Enter** or click and hold the mouse button.
4. Use the arrow keys or drag the mouse to stretch the rectangle to the desired size and shape.
5. Press **Enter** or release the mouse button.

Note

You also can draw a rectangle by clicking the Add a rectangle icon in the icon palette.

Draw Text

Purpose

Inserts a line of text at any location in the Graph window.

To insert text while in the Graph window

1. In the Graph window, select Draw Text by clicking the mouse or pressing **Alt+D+T** from the keyboard.
2. Type the characters you want to add to the graph and select **OK**.
3. Using the mouse or arrow keys, position the text in the desired location.
4. Click the mouse button or press **Enter**.

Note

You also can add text by clicking on the Add text icon in the icon palette.

Edit Copy

Purpose

Copies the entire contents of the Graph window to the Clipboard. You then can paste the graph in a Worksheet window or another Windows application.

To copy the contents of the Graph window to the Clipboard

1. In the Graph window, select Edit Copy by clicking the mouse or pressing **Alt+E+C** from the keyboard.
2. To insert the copied graph, go to a Worksheet window or another Windows application and select **E**dit **P**aste.

Edit Delete

Purpose

Removes the selected object(s) from the Graph window.

To remove an object from the Graph window

1. In the Graph window, select the object(s) to be deleted.
2. Select Edit Delete by clicking the mouse or pressing **Alt+E+D** (or **Del**) from the keyboard.

Note

You also can delete objects by clicking on the Delete permanently icon (a garbage pail) in the icon palette.

Edit Replicate

Purpose

Places a copy of the selected object(s) to the right and below the original.

The Edit Copy command copies the entire graph to the Clipboard so that you can insert it into a worksheet or another application; Edit Replicate copies an object within the Graph window.

To copy an object within the Graph window

1. In the Graph window, select the object(s) you want replicated.

2. Select Edit Replicate by clicking the mouse or pressing **Alt+E+R** (or **Shift+Ins**) from the keyboard.

Note

You also can duplicate objects by clicking on the Duplicate icon in the icon palette.

Edit Select

Purpose

Selects or unselects one or more objects in the Graph window. After objects are selected, you can delete, copy, rearrange, and format the objects.

To select an object in the Graph window

1. In the Graph window, choose Edit Select by clicking the mouse or pressing **Alt+E+S** from the keyboard.
2. Select one of the following options:

All	Selects all objects in the Graph window, except the underlying chart.
C**h**art	Selects the underlying chart.
Cycle	Cycles through all objects so that you can choose which objects to select.
None	Cancels the selection of all objects, leaving no objects selected.

3. If you chose **C**ycle, 1-2-3 places empty selection handles around the first object and presents a dialog box. Select from the following choices:

Option	*Description*
Next	Goes to next object.
Previous	Goes back to previous object.
Select	Selects current object.

4. Repeat step 3 for each object.

Edit Undelete

Purpose

Brings back the last object or group of objects you deleted. You can undelete objects deleted with (Graph window) Edit Delete, the Del key, or the Delete permanently icon.

To restore the last object deleted

In the Graph window, Select Edit Undelete by clicking the mouse or pressing Alt+E+U (or Ins) from the keyboard.

File Close

Purpose

Removes the current Graph window from the screen and makes the Worksheet window current.

To remove the current Graph window from the screen

In the Graph window, select File Close by clicking the mouse or pressing Alt+F+C from the keyboard.

File Exit

Purpose

Quits 1-2-3 and displays the Windows Program Manager. This command is identical to the Worksheet window's File Exit command. For more information, see *File Exit* in the Main Menu Command Reference.

Layout Fall Back

Purpose

Moves an object behind other objects in the Graph window.

To send an object behind other objects

1. In the Graph window, select the object(s) to position in the back.

2. Select Layout Fall Back by clicking the mouse or pressing **Alt+L+F** from the keyboard.

Note

You also can click the Place behind all other objects icon in the icon palette.

Layout Lock

Purpose

Protects an object from changes within the Graph window.

To protect an object

1. In the Graph window, select the objects to be locked.

2. Select Layout Lock by clicking the mouse or pressing **Alt+L+L** from the keyboard.

Layout Send Forward

Purpose

Moves an object in front of other objects in the Graph window.

To bring an object in front of other objects

1. In the Graph window, select the object(s) to be positioned in front.
2. Select Layout Send Forward by clicking the mouse or pressing **Alt+L+S** from the keyboard.

Note

You also can click the Place in front of all other objects icon in the icon palette.

Layout Unlock

Purpose

Makes changes to an object that was previously locked with the Layout Lock command.

To modify an object that was previously locked

1. In the Graph window, select the object(s) to be unlocked.
2. Select Layout Unlock by clicking the mouse or pressing **Alt+L+U** from the keyboard.

Rearrange Adjust Size

Purpose

Resizes the selected object(s) in the Graph window.

To resize an object in the Graph window

1. In the Graph window, select the object(s) to resize.
2. Select Rearrange Adjust Size by clicking the mouse or pressing **Alt+R+A** from the keyboard.
3. Use the arrow keys or the mouse to adjust the size.
4. Press **Enter** or click once.

Rearrange Clear

Purpose

Reverses all Rearrange commands that were performed on the selected object and returns the object to its original state.

To reverse all Rearrange commands

1. In the Graph window, select the object on which to reverse commands.
2. Select Rearrange Clear by clicking the mouse or pressing **Alt+R+C** from the keyboard.

Rearrange Flip

Purpose

Turns a selected object upside down, either horizontally or vertically.

To flip an object

1. In the Graph window, select the object(s) to flip.
2. Select Rearrange Flip by clicking the mouse or pressing **Alt+R+F** from the keyboard.
3. Select either **H**orizontal or **V**ertical.

Note

You also can click the Flip backwards or Flip upside down icon in the icon palette.

Rearrange Quarter-Turn

Purpose

Rotates selected object(s) in 90-degree increments.

To rotate an object

1. In the Graph window, select the object(s) to turn.
2. Select Rearrange Quarter-Turn by clicking the mouse or pressing **Alt+R+Q** from the keyboard.
3. Repeat step 2 until the object rotates to the desired position.

Rearrange Skew

Purpose

Changes the angles, size, and position of the selected object(s).

To modify the position of an object

1. In the Graph window, select the object(s) to skew.
2. Select Rearrange Skew by clicking the mouse or pressing **Alt+R+S** from the keyboard.
3. Use the arrow keys or the mouse to adjust the angles and size.
4. Press **Enter** or click once.

Rearrange Turn

Purpose

Rotates the selected object(s) to any angle.

To rotate an object

1. In the Graph window, select the object(s) to rotate.
2. Select Rearrange Turn by clicking the mouse or pressing **Alt+R+T** from the keyboard.
3. Use the arrow keys or the mouse to rotate the object(s).

4. Press **Enter** or click once.

Note

You also can click the Rotate icon in the icon palette.

Style Alignment

Purpose

Positions text with respect to the original location. Style Alignment works only with text added with Draw Text.

To align text

1. In the Graph window, select the text to align.
2. Select Style Alignment by clicking the mouse or pressing **Alt+S+A** from the keyboard.
3. Select **L**eft, **C**enter, or **R**ight.
4. Select **OK**.

Style Color

Purpose

Assigns colors to text, lines, object interiors, and the chart background.

To assign attributes

1. In the Graph window, select the text or object to be colored.
2. Select Style Color by clicking the mouse or pressing **Alt+S+C** from the keyboard.
3. To change the color of text, select a color from the **T**ext drop-down list.
4. To change the color of lines and object outlines, select a color from the **L**ine drop-down list.

5. To assign a color to the inside of an object, select a color from the Interior fill drop-down list.
6. To assign a color to the chart background, select a color from the Background drop-down list.
7. Select **OK**.

Style Display Options

Purpose

Controls how graphs are displayed on the worksheet. Style Display Options is available only if the graph has been inserted into a worksheet.

To display a graph on a worksheet

1. In the Graph window, select Style Display Options by clicking the mouse or pressing **Alt+S+D** from the keyboard.
2. Turn on or off one or more of the following check boxes:

Hidden	Displays a shaded rectangle in place of the added graph in the worksheet.
Show grid lines	Shows cell outlines in the Graph window.
Transparent	Enables you to see worksheet data underneath the added graph.
Updated automatically	Instantly revises the added graph when worksheet data changes.

3. Select **OK**.

Style Font

Purpose

Assigns a new typeface and size to added text. You can change the font of text added with the Draw Text command only.

To assign a new font

1. In the Graph window, select the text to format.
2. Select Style Font by clicking the mouse or pressing **Alt**+**S**+**F** from the keyboard.
3. From the **F**onts list, select a font.
4. To enlarge or reduce all text in the graph by the same percentage, select **M**agnify all fonts and enter a number between 1 and 1000.
5. Select **OK**.

Style Lines

Purpose

Formats the lines and outlines of objects added through the Draw menu. You can change the style of lines (such as solid or dashed), make the lines wider or narrower, add or reposition arrowheads, and smooth curves in an object.

To format the outline of an object through the Draw menu

1. In the Graph window, select the lines or objects to format.
2. Select Style Lines by clicking the mouse or pressing **Alt**+**S**+**L** from the keyboard.
3. Display the **S**tyle drop-down list and select one of the six line styles.
4. Display the **W**idth drop-down list and select one of the five line widths.

5. To place an arrowhead at the beginning of the line, turn on the Start of line option. To remove the arrowhead, turn this option on and then off.
6. To place an arrowhead at the end of the line, turn on the End of line option. To remove the arrowhead, turn this option on and then off.
7. For the smoothing options, select one of the following menu options:

Medium	Provides the maximum smoothing available; smooths the angles to a greater degree than the Tight option.
None	Returns a smoothed object to the original angles.
Tight	Slightly smooths or rounds the object's angles.

8. Select **OK**.

Tools SmartIcons

Purpose

Repositions the Graph window icon palette (for example, moves it to the left side of the window), selects the icons in the icon palette, and enables you to customize your own icons to add to the Graph window icon palette. For more information on this command, see *Tools SmartIcons* in the Main Menu Command Reference.

Window Cascade

Purpose

Functions the same way in the Graph window as in the Worksheet window. For more information, see *Window Cascade* in the Main Menu Command Reference.

Window Enlarge

Purpose

Zooms in on the center of the Graph window.

To zoom in on the center of a Graph window

In the Graph window, select Window Enlarge by clicking the mouse or pressing Alt+W+E (or +) from the keyboard.

Window Full

Purpose

Displays the entire contents of the Graph window. Use this command after you enlarge or zoom a particular area of the window.

To display an entire Graph window

In the Graph window, select Window Full by clicking the mouse or pressing Alt+W+F (or *) from the keyboard.

Window Reduce

Purpose

Reduces the size of the contents of the Graph window after the contents are enlarged.

To reduce the size of the contents in a Graph window

In the Graph window, select Window Reduce by clicking the mouse or pressing Alt+W+R (or –) from the keyboard.

Window Tile

Purpose

The Window Tile command functions in the Graph window exactly as it does in the Worksheet window. For more information, see *Window Tile* in the Main Menu Command Reference.

Window Zoom

Purpose

Selects the area to zoom in on and fills the window with the selected area.

To select an area to zoom

1. In the Graph window, select Window Zoom by clicking the mouse or pressing Alt+W+Z (or @) from the keyboard.
2. Use the mouse or arrow keys to position the crosshair pointer in the upper left corner of the area you want to zoom.
3. Press Enter or click and hold the mouse button.
4. Draw a box around the zoom area by pressing the arrow keys or dragging the mouse.
5. Press Enter or release the mouse button.

TRANSCRIPT WINDOW COMMAND REFERENCE

This Command Reference includes all the 1-2-3 for Windows commands that you can access from the Transcript Window. You access the Transcript Window by selecting Tools Macro Show Transcript from the Main menu.

Edit Clear

Purpose

Erases keystrokes from the Transcript window without moving the keystrokes to the Clipboard.

To erase keystrokes from the Transcript window

1. Highlight the keystrokes that you want to erase.
2. Select Edit Clear by clicking the mouse or pressing **Alt+E+E** (or **Del**) from the keyboard.

Note

You cannot undo the Transcript window's Edit Clear command.

Edit Clear All

Purpose

Erases all recorded keystrokes from the Transcript window without moving them to the Clipboard.

To erase recorded keystrokes from the Transcript window

Select Edit Clear All by clicking the mouse or pressing **Alt+E+R** from the keyboard.

Note

You cannot undo the Transcript window's Edit Clear All command.

Edit Copy

Purpose

Copies highlighted keystrokes from the Transcript window to the Clipboard, where they remain until you use Edit Paste.

To copy highlighted keystrokes from the Transcript window

1. Highlight the keystrokes you want to copy.
2. Select Edit Copy by clicking the mouse or pressing **Alt**+**E**+**C** (or **Ctrl**+**Ins**) from the keyboard.

Edit Cut

Purpose

Moves highlighted keystrokes from the Transcript window to the Clipboard, where they remain until you use Edit Paste.

To move highlighted keystrokes to the Clipboard

1. Highlight the keystrokes you want to cut.
2. Select Edit Cut by clicking the mouse or pressing **Alt**+**E**+**T** (or **Shift**+**Del**) from the keyboard.

Edit Paste

Purpose

Inserts the contents of the Clipboard at the cell pointer location.

To insert the contents of the Clipboard at the cell pointer location

1. Activate the window in which you want to paste the keystrokes.
2. If you are pasting to a worksheet, move the cell pointer to the area of the worksheet where you want the keystrokes to appear.

   If you are pasting to the Transcript window, move the cell pointer to the area of the window where you want the keystrokes to appear.

3. Select Edit Paste by clicking the mouse or pressing **Alt+E+P** (or **Shift+Ins**) from the keyboard.

File Close

Purpose

Removes the Transcript window from the screen.

To remove the Transcript window from the screen

1. Make sure that the Transcript window is active.
2. Select File Close by clicking the mouse or pressing **Alt+F+C** from the keyboard.

File Exit

Purpose

Quits 1-2-3 for Windows and displays the Windows Program Manager. For more information, see *File Exit* in the Main Menu Command Reference.

Macro Debug

Purpose

Displays the same dialog box as Tools Macro Debug and operates in the same way. For more information, see *Tools Macro Debug* in the Main Menu Command Reference.

Macro Minimize on Run

Purpose

Reduces the Transcript window to an icon and makes the window inactive while you play back keystrokes with Macro Run.

To change Transcript window to an icon

Select Macro Minimize on Run by clicking the mouse or pressing Alt+M+M from the keyboard.

Macro Pause Recording

Purpose

Suspends keystroke recording.

To suspend keystroke recording

Select Macro Pause Recording by clicking the mouse or pressing Alt+M+P from the keyboard.

Macro Run

Purpose

Plays back keystrokes from the Transcript window. In other words, this command executes the keystrokes as if these keystrokes were in a macro.

To play back keystrokes from the Transcript window

1. Highlight the keystrokes that you want to run as a macro.
2. Select Macro Run by clicking the mouse or pressing Alt+M+R from the keyboard.

Window

Purpose

Two Window commands are available in the Transcript window: Tile and Cascade. These commands function in the same manner in both the Transcript window and the Worksheet window. See the sections on Window commands in the Main Menu Command Reference.

The Window menu also offers a way to switch to other open windows. The names of the open windows appear at the bottom of the Window menu.

1-2-3 FUNCTIONS

For an in-depth discussion of 1-2-3 functions, see Que's *Using 1-2-3 for Windows*.

This section provides all 1-2-3 functions in alphabetical order.

@@(*cell_address*)

@ABS(*x*)

@ACOS(*angle*)

@ASIN(*angle*)

@ATAN(*angle*)

@ATAN2(*x,y*)

@AVG(*list*)

@CELL(*attribute,range*)

@CELLPOINTER(*attribute*)

@CHAR(*number*)

@CHOOSE(*offset,list*)

@CODE(*string*)

@COLS(*range*)

@COORD(*worksheet,column,row,absolute*)

@COS(*angle*)

@COUNT(*list*)

@CTERM(*interest,future_value,present_value)*

@DATE(*year,month,day*)

@DATEVALUE(*date_string*)

@DAVG(*input,field,criteria*)

@DAY(*date*)

@DAYS360(*start_date,end_date*)

@DCOUNT(*input,field,criteria*)

@DDB(*cost,salvage,life,period*)

@DGET(*input,field,criteria*)

@DMAX(*input,field,criteria*)

@DMIN(*input,field,criteria*)

@DQUERY(*external_function,*[*external_arguments*])

@DSTD(*input,field,criteria*)

@DSTDS(*input,field,criteria*)

@DSUM(*input,field,criteria*)

@D360(*start_date,end_date*)

@DVAR(*input,field,criteria*)

@DVARS(*input,field,criteria*)

@ERR

@EXACT(*string1,string2*)

@EXP(*x*)

@FALSE

@FIND(*search_string,string,start_number*)

@FV(*payments,interest,term*)

@HLOOKUP(*key,range,row_offset*)

@HOUR(*time*)

@IF(*test,true_result,false_result*)

@INDEX(*range,column,row*[*worksheet*])

@INFO(*attribute*)

@INT(*x*)

@IRR(*guess,cashflows*)

@ISAAF(*name*)

@ISAPP(*name*)

@ISERR(*cell_reference*)

@ISNA(*cell_reference*)

@ISNUMBER(*cell_reference*)

@ISRANGE(*cell_reference*)

@ISSTRING(*cell_reference*)

@LEFT(*string,number*)

@LENGTH(*string*)

@LN(*x*)

@LOG(*x*)

@LOWER(*string*)

@MAX(*list*)

@MID(*string,start number,number*)

@MIN(*list*)

@MINUTE(*time*)

@MOD(*x,divisor*)

@MONTH(*date*)

@N(*range*)

@NA

@NOW

@NPV(*interest,cashflows*)

@PI

@PMT(*principal,interest,term*)

@PROPER(*string*)

@PV(*payments,interest,term*)

@RAND

@RATE(*future_value,present_value,term*)

@REPEAT(*string,number*)

@REPLACE(*original _string,start_number,length, new_string*)

@RIGHT(*string,number*)

@ROUND(*x,precision*)

@ROWS(*range*)

@S(*range*)

@SECOND(*time*)

@SHEETS(*range*)

@SIN(*angle*)

@SLN(*cost,salvage,life*)

@SOLVER(*query_string*)

@SQRT(*x*)

@STD(*list*)

@STDS(*list*)

@STRING(*number,decimal_places*)

@SUM(*list*)

@SUMPRODUCT(*list*)

@SYD(*cost,salvage,life,period*)

@TAN(*angle*)

@TERM(*payment,interest,future_value*)

@TIME(*hour,minutes,seconds*)

@TIMEVALUE(*time_string*)

@TODAY

@TRIM(*string*)

@TRUE

@UPPER(*string*)

@VALUE(*string*)

@VAR(*list*)

@VARS(*list*)

@VDB(*cost,salvage,life,start,end,*[*depreciation*],[*switch*])

@VLOOKUP(*key,range,column_offset*)

@YEAR(*date*)

MACROS

Macros are text labels that automate the same keystrokes you enter when using 1-2-3. For example, the macro to widen a column's width to 12 characters is

{ALT}kc12~

Creating a Macro

Enter macros in three columns located below the worksheet's calculation area: one column for the macro's name (a reminder to the user), one column for the macro code, and one column to explain each line of the macro code.

To enter a macro manually

1. Move the cell pointer to an area away from the data area in the worksheet.
2. Use an empty cell to enter the macro name.
3. In a cell to the right of the name, enter the first macro instruction as a label.

4. Use the cells immediately below the first instruction to enter any subsequent instructions.
5. Use adjacent columns or an area below the end of the macro to enter subroutines and branch macros when necessary.
6. To end the macro, enter **{QUIT}** or leave a blank cell after the last line of the macro.
7. Highlight the macro name and use the Range Name Label Create commands to name the macro.

To create a macro with the Transcript window

1. Select Tools Macro Show Transcript.
2. Activate the Transcript window by clicking it with the mouse or pressing **Ctrl+F6** until the Transcript window is the active window.
3. To clear the Transcript window select Edit Clear All.
4. Activate the Worksheet window.
5. Run through the task you want to record select commands, type data, and move around the worksheet file or move interactively between worksheet files and other open windows.

To create a macro by copying keystrokes

1. Select Tools Macro Show Transcript.
2. Activate the Transcript window by clicking on it with the mouse or pressing **Ctrl+F6** until the Transcript window is the active window.
3. Select the recorded keystrokes you want to copy by dragging across the keystrokes while holding down the mouse. You also can use the navigation keys to move the I-beam to the first keystroke you want to select; then press and hold **Shift** and use the navigation keys to highlight the keystrokes.
4. From the Transcript window menu, select Edit Copy.
5. Activate the Worksheet window.
6. Highlight the first keystroke where you want to enter the first keystroke.

7. Select Edit Paste.
8. Highlight the macro name and use the Range Name Label Create command to name the macro.

Running a Macro

You can run a macro three different ways.

To run a backslash macro

Press **Alt+F3** (Run) or press **Ctrl** and the single-letter name.

To run a range-name or an unnamed macro

1. Select Tools Macro Run or press **Alt+F3** (Run).
2. Use the Macro name list box to select the macro name.
3. Select **OK**.

To run an auto-execute macro

Create the macro the regular way but name it **\ 0** (backslash zero).

1-2-3 executes the auto-execute macro when the file that contains it is opened. You can disable the auto-execute macros by selecting Tools User Setup, and clicking the Run autoexecute macros check box.

Debugging a Macro

You can debug a macro two different ways. The STEP mode executes the macro one instruction at a time; the TRACE mode opens a window that shows the current macro command and which step fails. Refer to *Tools Macro Debug* in the Main Menu Command Reference for more information.

Macro Key Names

Macro key names automate single- or multiple-key activities (for example, **Home**, **End**, or **Esc**), within macros. Using {HOME} in a macro, for example, moves the cell pointer to the upper left corner of the active window.

Use the following macro key names to perform certain key functions.

Macro Key Name	*Keyboard Key*
~	Enter
{ABS}	**F4** (Abs)
{ALT}, {MB}, or {MENUBAR}	**F10** (Menu)
{ANCHOR}	**F4** in READY mode
{APP1}	**Alt+F7** (App1)
{APP2}	**Alt+F8** (App2)
{APP3}	**Alt+F9** (App3)
{BACKSPACE} or {BS}	**Backspace**
{BACKTAB} or {BIGLEFT}	**Backtab** (**Shift+Tab**) or **Ctrl+←**
{BIGRIGHT}	**Tab** or **Ctrl+→**
{CALC}	**F9** (Calc)
{CLEARENTRY} or {CE}	Similar to **Esc**
{DELETE} or {DEL}	**Del**
{DOWN} or {D}	↓
{EDIT}	**F2** (Edit)

Macro Key Name	*Keyboard Key*
{END}	**End**
{ESCAPE} or {ESC}	**Esc**
{FILE}	**Ctrl+End**
{FIRSTCELL} or {FC}	**Ctrl+Home**
{FIRSTFILE}, {FF}or {FILE} {HOME}	**Ctrl+End Home**
{GOTO}	**F5** (GoTo)
{HELP}	**F1** (Help)
{HOME}	**Home**
{INSERT} or{INS}	**Ins**
{LASTCELL} or {LC}	**End Ctrl+Home**
{LASTFILE}, {LF} or {FILE} {END}	**Ctrl+End End**
{LEFT} or {L}	←
{MENU} or / or <	/ (slash) or < (less than)
{NAME}	**F3** (Name)
{NEXTFILE}, {NF} or {FILE}{NS}	**Ctrl+End Ctrl+PgUp**
{NEXTSHEET} or {NS}	**Ctrl+PgUp**
{PGDN}	**PgDn**
{PGUP}	**PgUp**

{PREVFILE} {PF} or {FILE}	**Ctrl+End Ctrl+PgDn**
{PREVSHEET} or {PS}	**Ctrl+PgDn**
{QUERY}	**F7** (Query)
{RIGHT} or {R}	→
{TAB}	**Tab**
{TABLE}	**F8** (Table)
{UP} or {U}	↑
{WINDOW}	**F6** (Pane)
{ZOOM}	**Alt+F6** (Zoom)
{~}	Tilde (for **Enter**)
{{}	Open brace
{}}	Close brace

Macro Commands

The advanced macro commands provide a programming language for developing custom applications in 1-2-3 for windows. Over 80 built-in advanced macro commands are available:

{subroutine}

{?}

{APP-ADJUST x,y,width,*height*}

{APPENDBELOW *destination,source*}

{APPENDRIGHT *destination,source*}

{APP-STATE}

{BEEP [*number*]}

{BLANK *location*}

{BRANCH *location*}

{BREAK}

{BREAKOFF}

{BREAKON}

{CLOSE}

{COMMIT [*driver*],[*database*]}

{CONTENTS *destination,source,*[*width*],[*format*]}

{DDE-ADVISE *location,item,*[*format*]}

{DDE-CLOSE}

{DDE-EXECUTE *string*}

{DDE-OPEN *application,topic*[*location*]}

{DDE-POKE *range,item*[format]}

{DDE-REQUEST *range,item*[*format*]}

{DDE-UNADVISE *item,*[*format*]}

{DDE-USE *number*}

{DEFINE *location1,location2,...location N*}

{DISPATCH *location*}

{EDIT-CLEAR [*selection*],[*property*]}

{EDIT-COPY [*selection*], [*format*]}

{EDIT-COPY-GRAPH}

{EDIT-CUT [*selection*], [*format*]}

{EDIT-PASTE [*selection*], [*format*]}

{EDIT-PASTE-LINK [*selection*], [*format*]}

{FILESIZE location}

{FOR *counter,start,stop,step,subroutine*}

{FORBREAK}

{FORM *input,*[*call-table*],[*include-keys*],[*exclude-keys*]}

{FORMBREAK}

{FRAMEOFF}

{FRAMEON}

{GET *location*}

{GETLABEL *prompt,location*}

{GETNUMBER *prompt,location*}

{GETPOS *location*}

{GRAPHOFF}

{GRAPHON [*named-graph*],[nodisplay]}

{IF *condition*}

{INDICATE [*string*]}

{LAUNCH *command*,[*window]*}

{LET *location,expression*}

{LINK-ASSIGN
name,range,[*property1*],[*property2*],[*property3*]}

{LINK-CREATE
name,application,topic,item,[*format*],[*mode*],[*location*]}

{LINK-DEACTIVATE *name*}

{LINK-DELETE *name*}

{LINK-REMOVE *name*}

{LINK-TABLE *location*}

{LINK-UPDATE *name*}

{LOOK *location*}

{MENUBRANCH *location*}

{MENUCALL *location*}

{ONERROR *branch*,[*message*]}

{OPEN *filename,access*}

{PANELOFF [*clear*]}

{PANELON}

{PUT *location,column,row,value*}

{QUIT}

{READ *bytecount,location*}

{READLN *location*}

{RECALC *location*,[*condition*],[*iterations*]}

{RECALCCOL *location*,[*condition*],[*iterations*]}

{RESTART}

{RETURN}

{ROLLBACK [*driver*],[*database*]}

{SETPOS *offset*}

{SYSTEM *command*}

{WAIT *time_number*}

{WINDOW-ADJUST *x,y,width,height*}

{WINDOW-SELECT *window*}

{WINDOW-STATE *state*}

{WINDOWSOFF}

{WINDOWSON}

{WRITE *string*}

{WRITELN *string*}

Index

D

G

H

I-J

S

T

U-V

W

X-Z